ISSUES IN JAPAN'S CHINA POLICY

The Royal Institute of International Affairs is an unofficial body which promotes the scientific study of international questions and does not express opinions of its own. The opinions expressed in this publication are the responsibility of the author.

The Institute and its Research Committee are grateful for the comments and suggestions made by Professor Gerald L. Curtis, Professor R. P. Dore, and Dr D. C. Wilson, who were asked to review the manuscript of this book.

ISSUES IN JAPAN'S CHINA POLICY

Wolf Mendl

New York
OXFORD UNIVERSITY PRESS

Published for
THE ROYAL INSTITUTE OF
INTERNATIONAL AFFAIRS

First published in the United Kingdom 1978 by
THE MACMILLAN PRESS LTD

First published in the U.S.A. 1978 by
OXFORD UNIVERSITY PRESS INC.
New York

ISBN 0-19-520031-4

Printed in Great Britain

To Takako

Red or white, China remains our next-door neighbor. Geography and economic laws will, I believe, prevail in the long run over any ideological differences and artificial trade barriers.

Shigeru Yoshida, 'Japan and the Crisis in Asia', *Foreign Affairs*, January 1951, p. 179

Contents

Preface and
Acknowledgements

WHEN Mr Tanaka followed President Nixon to Peking in 1972, his visit was surrounded by much speculation over the future course of Japan's foreign policy. The establishment of American relations with Peking opened a new era in east Asia. A diplomatic revolution had ended twenty-two years of American-Chinese confrontation. It was the climax of a series of developments which included the Soviet-American détente, the Sino-Soviet conflict, and the greater self-assertion of some of the west European states – France under de Gaulle and West Germany with its *Ostpolitik*. The international system was no longer dominated by the bipolarity of Soviet-American confrontation and a multipolar system had taken its place.

This was the widely held view of the early 1970s and Japan was counted among the poles or centres of influence in the new world order. How was this economic giant going to declare its interest and what was it going to do? The assumption was that, until then, Japan had had no foreign policy worthy of that description, that its policy had been to do as the United States did and to grow rich behind the protective shield of American military power in east Asia. It was often said that Japan now had to make choices, as if it had not made any choices since 1945. The same thing is still being said, by Japanese as much as outsiders.

To talk in these days of a country's 'choices', is to invite a great many objections. It is generally agreed that what passes as the foreign policy of a state is essentially the product of the interaction of many factors, among which perceptions of the national interest, the impact of the international environment, and the cyclical relationship between one country's actions and another's reactions are the most important.

Each of these factors raises further questions. For example, what do we mean by perceptions of the national interest? Do they not presuppose a perception of the nation? And whose perceptions are we talking about? We should certainly get a distorted view if we confined ourselves to those of the bureaucrats in the Foreign Ministry and a handful of politicians. Surely, one must include those of all the major interest groups which are concerned in one way or another with their country's external relations, and which may range from political parties and commercial enterprises to religious groups and the press.

The day-to-day actions of a government are the outcome of compromises between many different and competing interests. Over a period of time the more influential and persistent of those interests may impose a general direction on foreign policy. It is rare indeed that one can point to a towering figure, like Bismarck or de Gaulle, who has been able to impose a line of policy on his country.

It is therefore misleading to think of Japan's foreign policy in terms of clearly defined objectives consistently pursued. The processes of decision-making in a pluralist and open system, such as that of postwar Japan, usually end in the making of decisions designed to avoid explicit choice. The result may be a series of small steps which have the cumulative effect of some kind of choice, or it might be more accurate to speak of the establishment of a general trend or drift of policy.

This would be an appropriate description of the development of Japan's China policy since the war. In addition to the usual factors which govern the formulation of external policy, the student of Japan must take into account the extraordinarily well developed national self-awareness of the people – a product of the country's geography, history, and the fundamental cohesion of its society. Japanese and outsiders often refer to a 'crisis of identity' when discussing the problems of contemporary Japan, but what they mean may be misunderstood. The Japanese are very conscious of their 'Japaneseness' (if I may be forgiven for using the term). For them it is not a question of who they are, but a question of how they should relate to others.

In this connection, China has always had a significant place in the national consciousness : first as the source of East Asian civilization, of which the Japanese have fashioned a unique component; then as a power which tried at various times to make a proud and independent Japan accept its titular 'hegemony'; and in the past century as a vulnerable state in danger of falling under the influence of alien and hostile powers; more recently, after 1949, many Japanese saw China as a model for a resurgent Asia.

A distinction must be made, however, between the attraction of China for its own sake and attitudes towards China's communist ideology. Although intellectuals and students, in particular, were sympathetic to Marxism, others regarded it as a Western ideology and many among the ruling élites looked on it with fear. They preferred to see the Nationalist Chinese on Taiwan as the true representatives of 'eternal' China. Yet a fair number of 'conservative' Japanese were also drawn to mainland China in spite of rather than because of its communism. Economic interest naturally played a part in this but nationalistic and racial feelings were also involved.

Under the Occupation and in the 1950s, China played an important part in the Japanese search for identity in their relations with the United States. Emphasis on the long historical and cultural association and a sense of kinship with the Chinese helped many Japanese not to feel overwhelmed by the all-pervasive American presence and influence. The context of the 1960s and early 1970s changed this aspect of China in Japanese attitudes. American influence became less noticeable. The life-style and interests of the younger generation, many of whom had studied in the United States, were changing. China itself presented a confusing picture : on the one hand it had become a nuclear power, on the other it had plunged into the chaos of the Cultural Revolution. For the economically successful Japanese it was no longer a model, except for the ideologically committed.

In their dealings with China since 1972, the Japanese have faced many of the problems and difficulties which arise in the relationship of any two neighbouring states. Racial and cultural affinities do not render it any the easier – they may make the relationship still more difficult by injecting their own subtle complications into it. When we think of the future, we can no longer rely wholly upon past experience. The two national societies have developed along very different lines in the last thirty years – and very largely in isolation from each other. The potential for a close economic partnership exists but remains unfulfilled. Some of the old cultural bonds may no longer be so strong. China has the potential to become a superpower. Japan has become an economic power of global importance without military might. These are some of the factors which will shape Japan's China policy in the years ahead.

It is the purpose of this study to offer an interpretation of Japanese attitudes to China in the last thirty years and to explore the question whether they reveal the emergence of a distinctive Japanese policy towards China. The main body of the book takes the form of narrative chapters followed by chapters that analyse the issues of policy, as a moving film may be punctuated with stills. The last chapter takes a forward look and discusses some of the factors that will determine Japan's policy towards China.

The narrative is intended to provide a broad framework and not a detailed history. For the purpose of clarity I have grouped the issues under general headings, such as trade, Taiwan, security, domestic politics, etc. The categories overlap to some extent and their relative importance changes in the course of time. Thus, economic and commercial relations loom large in the years up to 1972, not because of their volume but because they were at the heart of the political relationship between the two countries. After 1972 the amount of trade increases considerably, yet bilateral political issues and Japan's relations with other countries assume a greater importance. The work is not written from the standpoint of a Japanologist. While recognizing the great importance of the domestic environment in the shaping of Japanese policy, it does not pretend to offer a detailed study of the processes in which China policy was formulated. Finally, since its primary concern is Japanese policy, I have tried to avoid any detailed discussion of the situation in China or of Chinese foreign policy. However, these subjects could not be ignored altogether and I have at various places introduced brief views of the Chinese side of things, though only in so far as they seemed necessary for an understanding of Japanese policy.

A grant from the Social Science Research Council enabled me to start work by spending six months in Japan. Many people have been involved subsequently, in one way or another, in the preparation of this book. I am very grateful for all their assistance, patience, and kindness. I hope they will not mind if I do not name them. However, I must mention a few who have taken a great deal of trouble to help me with the many difficulties I encountered.

Ronald Dore, Kunihiro Michihiko, Etō Shinkichi, Hosoya Chihiro, and Ichii Saburō read the whole or parts of the manuscript in the early stages of its gestation and made many valuable criticisms and suggestions. In the end product they may not recognize much of what they read at that time, but their contributions were none the less important, not least because they steered me away from many pitfalls. Ian Smart was of enormous assistance in the struggle to work out a satisfactory structure for the book. I am indebted to Rena Fenteman for her meticulous attention to all aspects of the manuscript. Andrew Lambert collected much useful information from material in the press library at Chatham House. Moriya Fumiaki and my wife translated Japanese language material. Norman and Margaret Marrow, friends for many years, compiled the index. In addition to typing the manuscript, my wife, as always, was a source of great encouragement.

My thanks go to all who have assisted me, likewise my apologies for not always following their good advice, which adds force to the author's customary assumption of full responsibility for all errors and shortcomings.

Watford, Herts
May 1977   W.M.

Abbreviations

ASEAN	Association of Southeast Asian Nations
ASPAC	Asian and Pacific Council
CHINCOM	China Committee
COCOM	Co-ordinating Committee
DSP	Democratic-Socialist Party
FEO	Federation of Economic Organizations
JCED	Japan Committee for Economic Development
JCP	Japan Communist Party
JSP	Japan Socialist Party
JT	*Japan Times*
JTW	*Japan Times Weekly*
KMT	Kuomintang
LDP	Liberal-Democratic Party
MITI	Ministry of International Trade and Industry
NHNA	*News from Hsinhua News Agency*
PRC	People's Republic of China
ROC	Republic of China
SCAP	Supreme Command Allied Powers
UNCTAD	United Nations Conference on Trade and Development

NOTE ON JAPANESE NAMES

Japanese usage, which is to place the family name before the given name, has been followed throughout the main text and the notes, except where quoted material follows the Western pattern.

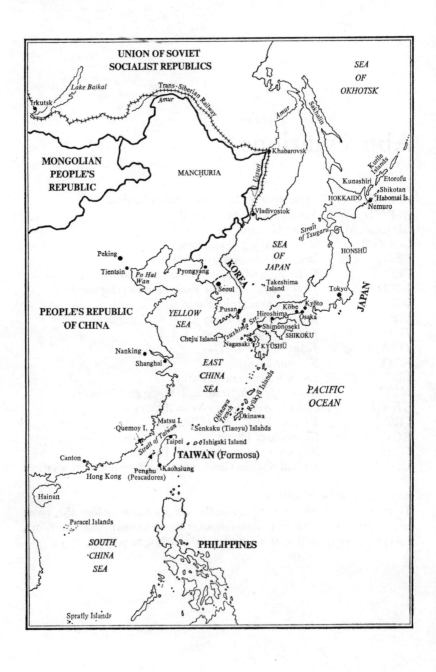

1 Japan's China Policy 1945–1971

WHAT might be called the postwar phase of Japan's relations with China was a long one, lasting for more than twenty-five years. It may be divided into four periods of almost equal length : the period of the Occupation, from 1945 to 1952; and three subsequent periods, respectively from 1952 to 1958, 1958 to 1965, and 1965 to 1971. Any division into historical periods, especially when the events are so recent, is bound to be rather arbitrary, but I have chosen this method so as to provide a chronological framework within which to focus more sharply on those issues which were to influence the development of Japanese attitudes and policies towards China in the 1970s.

During the first of these periods Japan had lost its independence and was under Allied (in fact, American) occupation. Under these conditions Japan had no official foreign policy. External relations were determined and controlled by the Occupation authorities. The Foreign Ministry (Gaimushō) was retained and it assumed a central position in the bureaucratic structure : among the reasons for this, its close contact with SCAP (Supreme Command Allied Powers) and Yoshida's doubling of the roles of Premier and Foreign Minister at the time of the negotiations over the Treaty of San Francisco (1951) and the Treaty of Peace with the Republic of China (1952), were the most important. In the early years of the Occupation, a Central Liaison Office was set up to handle relations between the Japanese government and Allied Headquarters. Apart from a brief period when it was made a department in the Office of the Prime Minister, it was to all intents and purposes a department of the Foreign Ministry and under the control of its minister.

The role of go-between for the Occupation authorities and the Japanese government, and the pro-American sympathies of Yoshida and many of the senior officials and advisers tended to make the Gaimushō identify Japan's basic external interests with those of the United States, an identification which continued long after 1952. Moreover, quite apart from the personal bias of key officials, it was clear that the Japanese authorities could take no decisions or action over their relations with the outside world without the approval of SCAP. It is therefore impossible to speak of an independent Japanese foreign policy at this time.

None the less, the period of occupation did not prevent the Japanese from thinking about and discussing the future course of their relations with China. Two influences played a major part in the formulation of a Japanese view of the China problem. One was the assumption that past experience would be relevant as a guide to future relations. The other and opposing influence was a growing awareness that things had changed fundamentally and called for an entirely new approach to China. This view gained in strength as it became obvious that the Communists were winning the civil war on the Mainland.

The Occupation may, therefore, be further divided into two periods. The first covers the years to 1949, during which there was a gradual readjustment in the Japanese view of China. The second covers the remaining three years until Japan achieved formal independence in 1952. The issues which were to dominate Japan's China policy in the following two decades emerged during these three years.

THE YEARS OF READJUSTMENT 1945–1949[1]

The sharp break in Japan's fortunes imposed by defeat and surrender ruptured the pattern of a relationship with China which had begun in the last quarter of the nineteenth century. That pattern consisted of a Japanese drive for domination in rivalry with other powers. It was cloaked in the argument that there was a special relationship between Japan and China because Chinese and Japanese belonged to the same racial and cultural family. In their competition with other powers for influence over China, the Japanese had convinced themselves that they had a particular claim to be at home in that country. High-sounding expressions of concern for the Chinese often merely covered predatory intentions and attitudes of contempt.

The apogee of this policy was reached with the military aggression of the 1930s and 1940s. Nevertheless, there had been an important group of people within the government, and even the army, which opposed military expansionism. They believed in Japan's mission to liberate east Asia from Western domination and to protect it against the threat of communism. They wanted a policy of co-operation with, rather than coercion of, the Chinese Nationalists, though they drew the line at Manchuria whose control was deemed to be essential for Japan's economy.[2]

Some of those who had been prominent and active in this group continued to play a part in public life after the war,[3] and their ideas influenced emerging attitudes towards China in the immediate post-war years. These attitudes included at least four aspects.

First, it was assumed that economic relations would continue to be of prime importance for Japan. Moreover, the great benefit of this relationship for China was not doubted. Prominent Japanese argued in October 1945 that the Chinese should allow the North China Economic Development Company to continue its operations because of the benefits it had conferred on China by providing employment and increased production of coal, salt, and other goods.[4]

Second, there was the search for reconciliation. Thus, for example, in September 1945 it was proposed to dispatch an 'Apology Mission' to be headed by Vice-Premier Prince Konoe. In 1948 Premier Ashida announced his intention to send a 'Friendship Mission' to China in the near future.[5]

Third, the Japanese readily supported the Kuomintang against the Communists. On 18 August 1945, four days after President Truman had received Japan's acceptance of unconditional surrender, the Commander-in-Chief of the Expeditionary Forces in China, General Okamura Yasuji, instructed his troops to co-operate in the reconstruction of China, to assist the Nationalist government in its efforts to unify the Chinese people, and to 'resolutely chastise' Communists if they displayed anti-Japanese behaviour. His meeting with the Vice-Chief of Staff of the Nationalist forces was reported to have been more like a conversation between friends co-operating against a common enemy than between victor and vanquished. Okamura continued to advise Chiang right up to the end of the civil war on the Mainland. Other Japanese officers also served the Nationalists, and Japanese troops fought against the Communists under the command of General Imamura for the Shansi warlord, Yen Hsi-shan.[6]

Finally, there were echoes of the concern to 'protect' China against the threat of domination by foreign powers. It stemmed from the traditional view that China's weakness was dangerous because it would invite interference by other powers, which might establish bases on the Mainland and threaten Japan.[7] At the time of the surrender, the Japanese warned the Chinese against the advance of Russia and urged them not to yield to the demands of 'outside powers'.[8]

The last two of these aspects were of considerable importance in influencing Japanese policy towards China in later years. Many of the ruling élites in postwar Japan retained close personal and ideological associations with the Chinese Nationalists. The victory of the Chinese Communists in 1949 and their close alliance with the Soviet Union in the 1950s confirmed the fear that China had fallen under the control of another power. However, the first aspect, the search for a renewal of the close economic relationship, turned out to be the most influential and remained so a quarter of a century later. Nevertheless, its frustration in the early years after the war awakened a realization among some that there had been a fundamental change in China's importance to Japan.

The contrast between the expectations and realities of trade in the first seven years of the postwar era was startling. Expectations were high because it was assumed that it would only be a matter of time before Japan-China trade reached its pre-war volume, which had accounted for approximately 25 per cent of Japan's total foreign trade. In fact, bilateral trade remained at a very modest level.[9]

The composition of the commodities reproduced the earlier pattern to some extent. Japan exported capital goods, three-quarters of which were metals and metal products. Machinery and transport equipment accounted for another 12 per cent. China exported agricultural, animal, and mineral products, including iron ore and coal. Seen in terms of percentages of Japan's total imports of a particular commodity, all the traditional imports from China were down on the pre-war figures :* coal : 58·8 per cent (68·4); iron ore : 18·7 per cent (34·0); soy-beans : 56·5 per cent (71·3); salt : 8·6 per cent (38·6). For the first time Japan had begun to import these commodities, except iron ore, from the United States. However, the American share of the total was very much smaller than the Chinese share, except in soy-beans.[10] The gross amounts and value of the postwar Japan-China trade were very small. By 1950 China took only 2·4 per cent of Japan's exports and provided 4 per cent of its imports, yet this was one of the peak years, the total value of the two-way trade having more than doubled in one year.

Three main constraints operated on trade in the early postwar period. They were the dislocation of the Chinese and Japanese economies, the policy of the Occupation authorities in Japan, and the ambivalent policy of Nationalist China. Matters were further complicated after 1949 by external and internal pressures for Japan to make a political choice between Taiwan and the Mainland.

Economic relations got off to a slow start, generally attributed to the wartime destruction of both countries. The Chinese civil war did not improve matters. In 1947 north China was unable to fulfil its role as supplier of salt because of the disruption of communications. There were hopes of a return to the traditional pattern when SCAP authorized the import of 250,000 tons of high-grade iron ore from Hainan in 1948; a small amount compared with the volume of iron ore imported before the war.[11]

---

* The first set of figures in each case is for 1950, those in brackets for 1934–6.

The second constraint could be attributed to American policies. The extent of the control exercised by the Occupation authorities was demonstrated in 1948. A mission to Nanking to discuss general aspects of Sino-Japanese trade did not list one Japanese among its members.[12] Later in the year, SCAP rejected an offer from the Kailan Mining Administration to barter Kailan coal for Japanese mining timber. The reason given was that Japan had to preserve its forests and needed three times as much timber as was available from domestic sources. Japanese traders and officials saw it differently. Japan needed coal more urgently than timber. They would have preferred to save valuable foreign exchange, spent on importing coal from the United States, by such a barter deal with China, especially as Chinese coal was much cheaper. The SCAP decision, despite an intervention by the Chief of the Chinese Mission in Tokyo, meant that Kailan would have to import timber from the United States or bring it from central China, both options being costly and time-consuming. The Japanese would have to continue spending their precious dollars on importing coal from the United States. Little wonder, then, that there were dark suspicions that the Americans were manipulating Japanese and Chinese needs to suit their own interests.[13]

The third constraint came from the course of Nationalist Chinese policy towards Japan. At the end of the war, Chiang Kai-shek was almost conciliatory. Referring to the people of Japan he said, 'We can only pity them because they have been so badly misled.'[14] In 1946 the official tone became hostile. The authorities opposed the flying of the national flag by Japanese ships in Chinese ports and made repeated demands for reparations.

The earlier friendly tone may be attributed to the need for Japanese co-operation in preventing a Communist take-over in large areas of north China and to the belief that Japanese managers and technicians would be needed to rebuild the economy. The apparent hostility which replaced it was a response to public opinion in China and not an indication of a change in economic policy towards Japan. On the contrary, the Nationalist Chinese representative on the Allied Council for Japan, which sat in Tokyo, consistently stressed the economic interdependence of China and Japan and pressed for policies which would hasten Japan's economic recovery for the benefit of both countries. Back home, however, there was widespread fear that the Americans were reviving Japan as an economic and military power. Popular demands, expressed through the political organs of Nationalist China, called for a strict limitation of Japanese industry, severe reparations, and the cession of the Ryukyus.[15]

CRYSTALLIZATION OF THE ISSUES IN JAPAN'S
CHINA POLICY 1949-1952

The real starting-point in the history of Japan's postwar relations with China was 1949. The next three years brought out all the major themes which have dominated the debate over policy towards China. The Communist victory on the Mainland cast further doubt about the future and importance of the economic relationship. Pressure from the United States during the negotiations over the peace treaty with the Allied powers forced the government to make a choice between the Nationalist Chinese on Taiwan and the Communist Chinese in Peking. The outbreak of the Korean War in 1950 turned attention to the problems of national security. Finally, the many conflicting interests involved in all these issues made the China question an important element in domestic politics.

Trade

Hopes were high that once unity and order had been restored on the Mainland there would be a very rapid and substantial increase in trade. Before the final Communist victory, preparations were afoot to set up a Japan-China Trade Promotion Council which claimed three hundred 'first-class firms' and some five hundred business leaders as its members. Such activities were reinforced by the views of the Minister of International Trade and Industry, Inagaki Heitarō, who spoke of long-range efforts to promote 25-30 per cent of Japan's import-export business with China.[16]

Other voices, notably that of Yoshida, struck a note of caution. The Prime Minister had made economic recovery the precondition of national independence but thought that Japan might get along without a heavy reliance on trade with China. He pointed to India, Pakistan, and Thailand as potential areas for trade expansion – countries which had not been exposed to Japanese military occupation and where anti-Japanese feelings were not strong.[17] SCAP, too, urged the Japanese to look elsewhere for trade outlets. Southeast Asia was considered to be one of the best prospects.

One would have thought that the outbreak and effects of the Korean War would have finally dispelled any illusions about an economic partnership with mainland China. Trade with the People's Republic fell to a very low ebb and was overtaken by trade with Taiwan.[18] American procurements for the war in Korea acted as a powerful stimulus to the Japanese economy and by 1952 Japanese overseas trade was flowing in new directions. None the less, the importance of the trade with China was to remain an article of faith for many Japanese.

The movement in its favour was especially strong in those regions, such as Kansai, which had traditional associations with the China trade, and in some industries which, for one reason or another, were unable to compete successfully in other markets.

In addition to these specialized interests, several other economic motives lay behind the drive for trade with China under the Occupation. Apart from the natural carry-over of thinking based on the pattern of economic relations in the pre-war decades, the importance of China appeared to be reinforced by the assumed impact of its industrialization policies over the next ten to fifteen years. It was argued that, unless trade with China revived, Japan would have to depend indefinitely on an annual American subsidy of approximately $500 million. It was also assumed that greatly increased trade with China would enable Japan to import Chinese coal at half the cost of American coal.

The Peace Treaties, the Two Chinas Policy, and National Security
The exceedingly complex negotiations leading to the conclusion of Japan's Treaty of Peace with the Republic of China illustrate Japan's reluctance to be cut off from the Mainland and to be wholly committed to American policy.

The Japanese government faced a dilemma. There were several very strong reasons for accepting the American position of uncompromising hostility to Communist China. Indeed, one could argue that it had little choice but to follow the American lead. The Allied powers were by no means united over which Chinese government to recognize. From the Japanese point of view, however, the United States was, so to speak, the power 'in possession'. To defy its wishes would have jeopardized the prospects of recovering national independence.

Another compelling reason why the Japanese did not wish to go against American policy was that they were negotiating simultaneously for a treaty of peace with the Allies and for a security treaty with the United States, both to be signed on the same day. The Japanese leaders, by and large, shared American perceptions of the international system that was emerging in the early Fifties. The war in Korea, a region about which the Japanese have always been very sensitive, seemed to confirm the seriousness of the Communist threat, which was seen as having two facets : subversion in Japan, promoted by a revolutionary Communist party; and an external threat from an expansionist Russia which dominated the Communist world, to which China had been added. Because Japan was unarmed, it was essential to ensure American protection against the external threat.

Against these considerations one has to set a deeply held feeling that, sooner or later, Japan would have to come to terms with the

government which ruled mainland China and that it would be contrary
to the national interest to cut all ties with the newly established
People's Republic. These feelings had their roots in the physical close-
ness of China, as well as in historical, cultural, and racial awareness.
Nor was the ideological factor so all-important to the Japanese as it
was to the Americans at that time. Moreover, Japan's leaders had to
take account of the very considerable pro-mainland China sentiment
in the country, by no means confined to communists and socialists.

Japan eventually signed its peace treaty with the Nationalist Republic of China on 28 April 1952. But it did so with reservations which
left open the way for a distinctive policy, independent of American
policy. The two points over which the Japanese position differed subtly
from that of the United States concerned the status of Taiwan and the
existence of two Chinese governments. To understand these nuances,
it is necessary to make a brief digression.

Following the outbreak of war in Korea in June 1950, American
policy began to stress the indeterminate political status of Taiwan.[19]
It was American pressure which ensured that the status of Taiwan
remained unclear under the terms of the peace treaty signed between
Japan and many of the wartime Allies at San Francisco on 8 September
1951. Neither Chinese government was a party to this treaty. Chapter
II, article 2(b) states that 'Japan renounces all right, title and claim
to Formosa and the Pescadores.' There is no mention of the subsequent
status of the islands.[20]

From the Chinese side there has never been any doubt over Taiwan's
status. It is regarded as an integral part of China and the policies of
both Kuomintang and Communists have been directed to preserving
this status. Moreover, the Chinese case rests on historical and legal
precedent. On 9 December 1941 the government of the Nationalist
Republic of China formally declared war on Japan and denounced
all treaties with Japan, including the Treaty of Shimonoseki of 1895,
under which Taiwan was given to Japan. As far as they were concerned, this action restored Taiwan to China. Neither the Kuomintang
nor the Communists recognized the validity of the cession by the Treaty
of Shimonoseki, which they regarded as a concession to force.

The positions of the Nationalist Republic of China and of the
People's Republic of China differed only in emphasis. These differences
need not concern us here. It is sufficient to note that both Chinese
governments agree that there can be no doubt that Taiwan is a
province of China.

Those who take the Chinese (red and white) position argue that
the Cairo Declaration issued by Roosevelt, Churchill, and Chiang Kai-
shek on 1 December 1943, and subsequently confirmed by the 'Allied
Proclamation to Japan', issued at Potsdam on 26 July 1945, became an

international accord, legally binding on Japan and the Allied powers, as soon as Japan had accepted the Potsdam Declaration through the Imperial Rescript of 2 September 1945.

The Cairo Declaration stated that :

... Japan shall be stripped of all the islands of the Pacific which she has seized or occupied since the beginning of the First World War in 1914, and that all the territories Japan has stolen from the Chinese, such as Manchuria, Formosa, and the Pescadores, shall be restored to the Republic of China.[21]

Article (8) of the Proclamation of Potsdam reads as follows :

The terms of the Cairo Declaration shall be carried out and Japanese sovereignty shall be limited to the islands of Honshu, Hokkaido, Kyushu, Shikoku and such minor islands as we determine.[22]

Therefore, the renunciation of Formosa and the Pescadores by Japan in the Treaty of San Francisco was deemed to have been made in favour of China.

The terms of the Japan-Republic of China Peace Treaty of the following year – 1952 – were seen as confirmation of China's sovereignty over Taiwan (the text of the Treaty is given at Appendix B, below). They did not specifically clarify the status of Taiwan, but the wording could be interpreted as supporting its reversion to China. Article II states Japan's renunciation of all claims to the territory. In Article IV Japan recognizes that all treaties concluded between China and Japan before 9 December 1941 'had become null and void as a consequence of the war.' Finally, Article X defined the nationals of the Republic of China in language which included all the inhabitants of Taiwan.

Those who were inclined to take the American view maintained that the status of Taiwan had become indeterminate and they later used this to bolster the call for the island's self-determination. In their opinion, the Chinese termination of treaties with Japan in 1941 had no legal effect because international agreements may not be abrogated unilaterally. Next, the basic assumption of the Cairo Declaration that the people of Taiwan wanted to become a part of China could be challenged on the grounds that the Chinese civil war and its aftermath had created a new situation.

According to the principles of self-determination embodied in the UN Charter, the people's aspirations had to be taken into account. There was no proof that Chiang's government represented the will of the Taiwanese, as it had not been elected by them. Where there is a conflict between the obligations of a member state under international agreements and under the Charter of the United Nations, the Charter takes precedence according to Article 103. The Declarations of Cairo and Potsdam merely reflected the wartime objectives of the four Allied powers. They were not specifically embodied in the peace treaties of 1951 and 1952 and therefore have no legal validity. The Chinese Nationalists had been asked to accept the Japanese surrender on Taiwan on behalf of the Allied powers. Strictly speaking, therefore, the Kuomintang exercised control over Taiwan as a government in exile administering a former colonial territory of Japan on behalf of the Allies.

Thus, the difference between Japan and the United States in the early Fifties was that the Japanese position left no doubt that Taiwan belonged to China, whereas the American position, while never explicitly denying this, was such as to leave room for argument that Taiwan might in future be regarded as a separate entity. The second, more important, difference was over the existence of two Chinese governments.

The United States government was anxious to prevent any agreement between Japan and Communist China at a time when the Chinese were engaged in open hostilities in Korea. The opposition of leading Republican senators to any Japanese *rapprochement* with the government in Peking gave strong leverage to Mr Dulles, the special Presidential Envoy charged with negotiating the San Francisco Peace Treaty and the bilateral security pact between the United States and Japan. If the Japanese made any moves towards Peking, then the Senate might not ratify the treaty to be signed at San Francisco. The point was brought home by the visit to Tokyo of two senior senators, one from each party, and by the letter sent by fifty-six senators of both parties to President Truman immediately after the signing of the Treaty of San Francisco, declaring that :

> Prior to the submission of the Japanese treaty to the Senate, we desire to make it clear that we would consider the recognition of Communist China by Japan or the negotiating of a bilateral treaty with the Communist Chinese regime to be adverse to the best interests of the people of both Japan and the United States.[23]

This was the background of the celebrated Yoshida Letter of 24 December 1951 (see Appendix A, below). It was the Japanese government's declaration of intent and began significantly by insisting that the ultimate objective was to have 'political peace and commercial intercourse with China'. For the present, it hoped to establish formal relationships with the National government of the Republic of China because of its status in the United Nations and its recognition by most members of that organization.

The Japanese promised to sign a treaty with the government in Taipei for the normalization of relations between the two governments. The treaty would apply to areas under the present or future control of the Republic of China. Japan had no intention of concluding a bilateral treaty with the régime in Peking. The reasons given for this last assurance were the branding of the Communist government as an aggressor by the UN;[24] the conclusion of the Sino-Soviet Treaty of Friendship, which was 'virtually a military alliance aimed against Japan'; and Peking's support for the Japan Communist Party (JCP).

Thus, while the Japanese followed the American line, they left the way open for changes in policy by limiting their engagement to the territories under the control of the government in Taipei, by tying their action to the main current of international opinion as expressed in resolutions of the United Nations, and by holding out the possibility of full or partial accommodation with Peking in the future, provided certain conditions were met. These included alteration or weakening of the Sino-Soviet alliance and a break with the JCP. Both had occurred by the 1970s. In theory, at least, any change in Japanese policy would not, therefore, be dependent on a change in American policy.

According to American sources, no pressure was involved. Mr Yoshida was perfectly willing to make the statement. He had asked Mr Dulles to let him have a draft of a declaration which could be used to persuade the senators that Japan had no intention of coming to terms with the government in Peking. When it was submitted to the Japanese they made some changes in the text and the letter was duly released. It served its purpose because the matter of Japan's future relations with the People's Republic of China hardly featured in the subsequent Senate Hearings. The two senators who had been to Tokyo were exceedingly anxious to establish that there had been no pressure on the Japanese. Their intention was to allay the suspicions of the British government, which regarded the letter as a betrayal of the Anglo-American agreement to allow Japan a free hand over its choice of relations with the two Chinese governments. The feelings of the Japanese were hardly considered.[25]

The Japanese government had, in fact, decided to normalize relations with the government in Taiwan before Mr Dulles' first visit to Tokyo in January 1951. It had been alarmed by the tone of the Sino-Soviet Treaty of Friendship, Alliance and Mutual Assistance, whose first article was directed specifically against Japan. The outbreak of the Korean War had increased anxiety over security and strengthened the Japanese in their conviction that it could be guaranteed only by the United States. Moreover, Mr Yoshida had been a member of the 'Anglo-American Faction' in the Foreign Ministry, which had long insisted that Japan's destiny lay in good relations with the great naval powers of the Pacific.

In spite of the reasons why Japan should have preferred to establish relations with the government in Taipei, an unequivocal alignment with the Nationalist régime was not considered to be in its best interests. Leaving aside his sympathies for the United States, Mr Yoshida was conscious of the ultimate realities in Asia. His reservations were strengthened by a general feeling in the Liberal and Democratic Parties, which formed the basis of support for the postwar conservative governments until their merger as the Liberal-Democratic Party (LDP) in 1955, that favoured keeping lines open to Peking. There was considerable misgiving over the need to make a choice between one or other of the Chinese régimes. On 22 May 1952 Foreign Minister Okazaki Katsuo told the House of Representatives Budget Committee that the Yoshida Letter did not bind successor governments, that it represented Mr Yoshida's opinions and should not be regarded as an international pledge.[26]

The negotiations which led to the conclusion of the Japan-Republic of China Treaty of Peace in April 1952 and its terms illustrate Japanese ambivalence over China and the desire to keep open as many options as possible for a more independent policy in the future.

The Japanese wanted a treaty to *normalize* relations between the two governments. In international law, war is a relation between states and not governments. Hence, a treaty between governments would not have had the legal effect of ending the war between Japan and China. This would have left open the way for eventual negotiations with the government on the Mainland. The Nationalist Chinese naturally wanted a *peace treaty* with its implied recognition that they were the only government representing the state of China. A similar problem arose thirteen years later over the normalization of Japan's relations with the Republic of Korea.

When it came to signing the Treaty (see Appendix B, below), on 28 April 1952, the Japanese had yielded over the nomenclature and agreed to a peace treaty. This was due to pressure from Mr Dulles and the threat of Congressional refusal to ratify the Treaty of San Francisco. The Nationalists had proposed twenty-one articles, almost identical to the Treaty of San Francisco. The Japanese submitted a briefer six-point document which omitted all matter referring to the Mainland and reparations. In the event, they settled for fourteen articles and a protocol.

The Japanese wanted to avoid the issue of reparations because it would further close the door to future negotiations with the Mainland

and because it might weaken their position *vis-à-vis* other countries which had already made claims. In the Diet debate over the Treaty, a government spokesman said that the question of reparations did not concern Taiwan but the Mainland. The Nationalists, however, persuaded the Japanese to recognize the principle of reparations, i.e. by referring to them in the text, but, as a 'sign of magnanimity', waived their claim in section 1(b) of the protocol.

The territorial issue was the most critical one in the negotiations. In the Yoshida Letter, Japan proposed that the terms of the Treaty should apply to 'all territories which are now, *or* (my italic) which may hereafter be, under the control of the National Government of the Republic of China'. The Kuomintang demanded that 'or' should be replaced by 'and'.

The final version of the Treaty left the territorial definition rather confused. The English text, which was definitive, mentions China in three different ways. Articles I (terminating the state of war), VI (setting out the principles of co-operation between the two countries), VII (referring to a commercial and maritime treaty), VIII (referring to a civil aviation agreement), IX (referring to a fishing agreement), and XI (referring to the settlement of problems resulting from the state of war), speak of the Republic of China. Articles III (referring to the disposition of property and claims) and X (defining nationals of the Republic of China), delimit the Republic of China as Taiwan (Formosa) and Penghu (the Pescadores). Articles IV (referring to treaties, conventions, and agreements before 1941) and V (referring to Japan's renunciation of special rights and interests), refer to China.

In the protocol, 1(a) speaks of the 'territories of the Republic of China' and 1(b) waives the right of the Republic of China to reparations. 2(d, i) defines the registration of vessels and the products of the Republic of China as those of Taiwan and Penghu.

These terminological obscurities were a mixed blessing for Japan. Their imprecision offered some freedom of manœuvre in future negotiations with the Mainland, but they also turned out to be a source of embarrassment to the Japanese government when it sought to establish relations with Peking.

The Treaty was denounced by the Chinese Communist government, which reserved the right to demand an indemnity from Japan. It was this problem which largely drove successive Japanese governments into arguing that the question of reparations had been settled once and for all, thereby reversing the original Japanese policy.

The issue arose first in 1959 over reparations for Vietnam. The government maintained that the agreement with the authorities in Saigon covered both the northern and southern halves of the country. Questioning in the Diet revealed that a similar meaning was applied to reparations concerning China. The terms of the Treaty between Japan and Nationalist China were thus interpreted as extending to all of China. Yet, in spite of the shift of emphasis, successive governments still insisted on maintaining *de facto* relations with the Mainland and recognizing a state of civil strife in China, as implied by the territorial restrictions of the Treaty.

In effect, Japan had tried to put an end to the state of war between the two countries while reserving for itself a free hand for future dealings with the Mainland. The innumerable difficulties which beset Sino-Japanese relations afterwards arose from the ambiguous policy embarked upon in 1952. It drove Japan into many contradictions and exposed it to pressures and retaliation from both Chinese governments. It also distinguished Japanese policy from American policy.

The events surrounding the Japan-Republic of China Treaty brought to the surface a two Chinas policy. This became the answer to the inability of Japan's ruling group to achieve a unified view of China policy and partly reflected a diplomatic objective : to keep options open for the time of change which would surely come one day. From 1952 onwards the theme of two Chinas runs through Japanese policy. Sometimes openly, sometimes hidden, but always there, it became the object of dispute and manœuvre within the government and symbolized independence from American policy.

The development of Japan's China policy between 1950 and 1952 cannot be separated from the problem of security. The Japanese authorities generally shared the American perception of a Communist threat, hence the necessity for a security treaty with the United States. But from the beginning they had a somewhat different idea about its purpose. They saw it as an essential guarantee against a potential enemy – the Soviet Union. China was not perceived as a threat by itself, but as a satellite in the Soviet system. While the Japanese were prepared to offer facilities so that the United States could perform its role of defending a disarmed Japan, they did not see themselves as partners in the task of ensuring the security of east Asia and certainly not as taking part in a great crusade against communism.

Thus, while Japan felt the need for American protection, it did not take an unequivocally hostile view of the People's Republic of China. This ambivalent attitude towards the Chinese Communists was partly due to the exigencies of domestic politics.

The China Question in Domestic Politics
The economic motives behind the pressure for relations with mainland China have already been mentioned. China policy had also become an important issue in Japanese politics because it was a symbol of the drive for national independence. The desire for independence was

probably universal, but there was a basic difference over perspectives. There were those, including right-wing conservatives and left-wing radicals, who sought national independence in an independent policy towards China and an autonomous security policy (some favoured rearmament, some unarmed neutrality). Others, including Yoshida, gave priority to economic reconstruction, with external security guaranteed by the United States.

The opposition parties' campaign against the government's policy of leaning towards the Kuomintang was a nationalist phenomenon. Admittedly, its socialist and communist leaders expressed themselves in Marxist terms, but their appeal was to Japanese nationalism. Attacks against subservience to American policies over China were calculated to arouse the same response as campaigns against nuclear weapons, which had first been unleashed by white Americans against Asians.

The ruling circles were divided over China policy. Even the government did not speak with one voice.[27] Japan had to accept the American connection, but there was general agreement that this should not mean identification with the United States over China. The differences arose over the best way in which to approach the China question. There were those who were committed to Taiwan through a mixture of romantic nostalgia, past associations, material interests, and, in the case of some prominent politicians and industrialists, close relations with the Kuomintang. There were others whose sentiment, associations, and commercial interests inclined them towards the Mainland and a search for accommodation with the new government there.

Another line of division ran between those, like Yoshida, who were 'nationalists' without making a sharp distinction between white or yellow nations, and those whose nationalism had strong racial overtones. Yoshida and his followers were perfectly willing to co-operate with the United States without equating Japanese and American interests in every respect or permanently. The second group, which included Matsumura Kenzō, a prominent conservative politician and an exponent of relations with Peking, stressed the ties of kinship between Japanese and Chinese in contrast to the 'strangeness' of the Americans.

The course of events of the Occupation period, particularly during the last three years, revealed both the underlying drive to develop an independent Japanese policy towards China and the constraints which prevented this development. Although Japan was officially under *Allied* occupation, the predominant role of the United States meant that Japan had to comply with American policies. It did so unenthusiastically and with a number of tacit reservations. The only way in which

Japan could assert its independent approach to the China question was by seizing whatever opportunities were available for keeping open communications with the Mainland and for retaining options for the future.

The strong interest in trade with the Mainland, the attempt to avoid signing a *peace* treaty with the government of Chiang Kai-shek, the wish to leave the question of reparations unsettled, the periodic statements, as in the Yoshida Letter, of the ultimate intention to establish normal relations with China, and the differences with the United States over the status of Taiwan and the recognition of the People's Republic of China all underline the existence of a distinctive Japanese approach to the China problem. The frustration of Japanese objectives cannot, however, be laid at the door of the United States alone. Indeed, the differences from the American position which did emerge in 1952, suggest that Japan might have succeeded in establishing its own line of policy if there had not been constraints other than the American domination of Japan.

One set of such constraints was provided by Chinese policy and by the international environment, which came to be dominated by the confrontations of the Cold War. Once in power, the Chinese Communists turned out to be uncooperative and hostile. Their domestic economic policies and their close ties with the Soviet Union left little scope for the development of Sino-Japanese trade. The Sino-Soviet Treaty of Friendship, openly directed against Japan, and Chinese intervention in the Korean War, made it impossible to think of establishing a friendly political relationship with the government in Peking. Finally, and most important, there was the problem of two Chinese governments. Neither was prepared to allow Japan to separate economics from politics in its relations with the Mainland.

The other set of constraints arose out of the political situation in Japan. Both parties to the Chinese civil war had their Japanese sympathisers. Those who supported the Kuomintang were the more influential, but the cross-currents of economic interest, the perceived importance of China for Japan's future, and the appeal to a latent nationalism of an independent China policy, combined to moderate an official leaning towards the Kuomintang.

The four themes which were to dominate Japan's relations with China in the next twenty years, had emerged clearly by 1952. They were trade, the 'two Chinas' policy, the problem of security and the international environment, and the place of the China question in domestic politics.

Before we turn to an analysis of these issues in the next chapter, a brief chronological survey of the evolution of Japanese policy towards China from the end of the Occupation to 1971 may be useful. (The reader is also invited to refer to the comparative chronology, at Appendix E below, for a list of the principal events.)

A bird's-eye view of the flow of events over the twenty years after 1952 reveals a kind of cyclical pattern which may be divided into three periods, each beginning with a gradual build-up of the relationship with mainland China and culminating in a crisis. In order not to lose sight of the themes in Japan's China policy, I will subdivide each cycle into three sections. The first deals with the international background, next comes the evolution of commercial relations, and finally there is a glance at the political issues which turn around the existence of two Chinese governments.

CYCLE I : 1952–1958

The International Background
When Japan signed the Treaty of Peace with the Republic of China, the Korean War was still in progress though slowly grinding to the halt which came with the armistice in 1953. The middle 1950s saw the first signs of a thaw in the Cold War. In June 1954 Chou En-lai and Jawaharlal Nehru published the Five Principles of Peaceful Co-Existence. The following year, 1955 – the year of Bandung, of the Austrian State Treaty, of the Geneva Conference on the Peaceful Uses of Atomic Energy, and of the initiation of ambassadorial talks between the United States and the People's Republic of China – seemed particularly propitious. However, it was a false dawn. By 1958 the international climate had again become harsher. In east Asia the situation was sombre, with heightened tensions between the United States and Red China in the Strait of Taiwan.

Trade Relations
The pattern of trade with the Mainland was set almost immediately after the signing of the peace treaty with the Nationalist régime on Taiwan. On 1 June 1952 the first unofficial trade agreement was signed in Peking. A business-like document, it had neither preamble nor protocol and made no mention of political issues. It established a system of barter trade.[28] In September, Japan joined the newly established CHINCOM, the inter-allied committee which controlled trade with Communist China.[29] Henceforth, Japan's trade with the Mainland was beset by conflicting pressures. On the one hand were the restrictions – and Chinese counter-measures[30] – as a result of Japan's political associations with the United States and the Chinese Nationalists. On the other hand, trade with the Chinese Communists was fostered and promoted by interested parties in Japan and assiduously encouraged

by Peking. For instance, in July 1953, the House of Representatives of the Japanese Diet unanimously passed a resolution calling for the development of Sino-Japanese trade as the first step towards improving relations between the two countries. The resolution was re-adopted three years later.

Between 1952 and 1958 four unofficial trade agreements were signed. They were strongly backed by a supra-partisan Diet Members' League for the Promotion of Sino-Japanese Trade, which included some influential members of the government party. Japanese exports were always well below the target set by each of the agreements, largely because of the embargo. Imports were also well below the objective, except for those under the third agreement.[31]

Commercial relations were further strengthened by the inauguration of annual trade fairs between the two countries. The first Chinese sample fair was held in Tokyo and Ōsaka during the last quarter of 1955. The Japanese exhibited in Peking and Shanghai in the following year. Nor was encouragement lacking from the Chinese side. In 1957 they expressed interest in buying twenty-five plants, covering a variety of industries and worth $400 million in all, to further the objectives of their second Five Year Plan.

Political Issues

An interesting pattern of official ambivalence over relations with Communist China began to emerge as soon as Japan had achieved its independence. Candidates for the office of prime minister invariably hinted at a policy of increased trade and generally improved relations. Equally invariably these policies, especially that concerning an improved political relationship, were left largely unfulfilled.

Yoshida had, of course, wanted to leave the lines to Peking open, but little movement could be expected under his premiership after he had steered through the treaties which tied Japan officially to the Nationalist government and to the alliance with the United States.

His successor in 1954, Hatoyama Ichirō, was expected to take a new line, partly because of his bitter political and personal animosity towards Yoshida. After his first cabinet meeting he said that he was not worried about American anxieties about his interest in trade with the Soviet Union and People's China. Trade would prevent the outbreak of world war three, but this did not mean siding with the Communist bloc against the West.[32] In March 1955 he told a press conference that he wanted to see a solution to the China problem on the basis of accepting both Chinas.[33] In the end, however, Hatoyama put his main effort into normalizing relations with the Soviet Union, which he achieved on 19 October 1956. Indeed, this appeared to have been done independently of the problem of relations with China. Hatoyama's freedom of manœuvre was severely restricted by the absence of any agreement within the ruling party over China policy, other than the desirability of increased trade.

When Ishibashi Tanzan succeeded Hatoyama in December 1956, it was reasonable to expect an improvement in the relations with Peking. Ishibashi was a businessman, well known for his associations with, and sympathies for, the People's Republic of China. However, illness forced him to retire two months later and the next Prime Minister, Kishi Nobusuke, was equally well known for his sympathies for the Kuomintang. Yet, Kishi too favoured an expansion of trade relations with mainland China and during his first days in office did not give the impression that his views differed much from those of his predecessor.[34]

All this was to change when Kishi visited Taiwan in the summer of 1957, the first Japanese prime minister to do so since independence. It was reported that he had encouraged Chiang Kai-shek to consider embarking on the reconquest of the Mainland. The climax that marked the end of the first cycle in Japan's relations with China was not long in following.

The fourth unofficial trade agreement had been signed on 5 March 1958, after protracted and difficult negotiations. It recognized the right of both parties to fly their national flags over their trade missions. This immediately raised the question whether it implied Japanese recognition of the People's Republic of China. Under strong pressure from Chiang Kai-shek and his supporters in Tokyo, the Japanese government made it clear that the flying of flags had no legal significance and that the Chinese trade mission enjoyed no official or diplomatic privileges. The signature of the trade agreement did not imply any recognition of the People's Republic. On 2 May 1958 a Japanese youth tore down the Communist Chinese flag from an exhibition in Nagasaki. Eight days later the Chinese Communists severed all trade relations with Japan. In June they refused to renew a fisheries agreement which expired that month.[35]

CYCLE II : 1958–1965

The International Background
The beginning of the second cycle of relations with the Mainland took place against a threatening background. The 1960 summit meeting in Paris broke up in disorder and ended with Khrushchev's pavement press conferences. The following year witnessed the Berlin Crisis, which turned out to be a prelude to the even more severe crises in the autumn of 1962 when Russia and the United States were in confrontation over

the missiles in Cuba, and India and China engaged in a frontier war. All these events masked fundamental shifts in the pattern of international relations which came to the surface with China's fierce and open polemics against Soviet 'revisionism' in 1960, and, in the Western camp, with de Gaulle's independent policies.

The Sino-Soviet conflict, which the Chinese date from 1956, the year of Khrushchev's attack on Stalinism and of the troubles in Poland and Hungary, had an important impact on Japan's relations with China. Its significance was not perceived for some time. For example, a conference of Japanese ambassadors in the summer of 1958 was perplexed by the contrast in Soviet and Chinese policies towards Japan : the Soviet Union was conciliatory while China was very hostile. However, the ambassadors concluded that the policies of both countries were consistent with each other.[36]

By the early 1960s, however, the rift between the two communist giants was beginning to affect Japanese assessments of relations with China. It was no longer possible to see China and Russia as belonging to one monolithic bloc. Within the ruling Liberal-Democratic Party (LDP) there developed a difference of opinion between those who wanted to use the conflict as an opportunity to isolate China and those who wanted to exploit the situation by drawing China into the Western camp. The official line was to wait and see.[37]

The Japanese had also been made aware that China's break with the Soviet Union might confer considerable economic benefits on themselves. The Russians had cut off all economic assistance and withdrawn their technicians, leaving many projects unfulfilled. When Takasaki Tatsunosuke, a businessman with pre-war associations with China and now a prominent member of the LDP, visited China in October 1960, the Chinese allowed him to go to Manchuria and China's northeast provinces. Takasaki noticed the various projects which had never got off the ground or had been left unfinished because of the break with the Soviet Union. There is no doubt that he and Japanese industrialists saw in this an opportunity for Japanese enterprises.[38]

One other event in east Asia had an important influence on Japanese thinking. France established diplomatic relations with Peking on 19 January 1964. Apart from the immediate effect of this on Japanese attitudes it also had a longer-term significance. De Gaulle's nationalism appealed to those Japanese not committed to socialism or communism but who disliked Japan's close and subordinate relations with America. De Gaulle had made recognition of Peking respectable (the much earlier British recognition of 1950 had been overshadowed by China's subsequent intervention in the Korean War and by Britain's co-operation with American policies). Those advocating such a step could no longer be dismissed as communist dupes or subversives.

Trade Relations

In August 1958 Premier Chou En-lai promulgated three principles ('demands' from the Japanese point of view) for the normalization of Sino-Japanese relations : (1) the Japanese government must cease its hostility to the PRC in word and deed; (2) it must stop plotting to create two Chinas; (3) it must refrain from obstructing the normalization of relations between Japan and Communist China. Although these were conditions for the establishment of political relations, their explicit acceptance became the test for any Japanese firm which wanted to trade with China.

Japan's trade with China was a mere trickle in 1959 and 1960 and it improved only gradually in the following years. Exactly two years after he had formulated the principles for the normalization of relations with Japan, Chou established three categories for the conduct of trade with Japan : (1) trade guaranteed by official agreements between the two governments; (2) trade by contract between Japanese firms and Chinese corporations; (3) trade specially designed to assist those businesses which depended on China for their supply of raw materials – an encouragement to the pro-China lobby among medium and small enterprises.

Chou's categories became the basis of a two-tier system of trade between the two countries, which dominated economic relations until the normalization of relations in 1972. The two tiers were respectively named 'Memorandum Trade' and 'Friendly Trade'.[39] The original trade memorandum was negotiated in 1962 by Liao Cheng-chih, a member of the Central Committee of the Chinese Communist Party who was prominent in the conduct of the Party's external relations, and Takasaki Tatsunosuke. In the early years it was known as L-T Trade, from the initials of the two principal negotiators. Later it became Memorandum Trade (MT) when the agreement was periodically renegotiated. 'Friendly Trade' was regulated under a protocol to the original L-T Agreement.

The Japanese side was anxious to make clear that the agreements were not signed by representatives of the government, and, therefore, had no official character. The negotiators were usually senior and influential members of the LDP, sympathetic to the People's Republic of China. They justified the formal agreements as a means to prevent disorderly competition among Japanese traders and to strengthen their bargaining position *vis-à-vis* the rigidly and centrally controlled Chinese.

It is quite clear, however, that both the Chinese and the Japanese who negotiated Memorandum Trade intended it as a channel for promoting inter-governmental relations. Despite Japanese protestations to the contrary, the trade offices which were later established in Peking and Tokyo gradually assumed the character of semi-official missions. Bureaucrats from the Ministry of International Trade and Industry (MITI), and not long afterwards from the Foreign Ministry as well, served unofficially in the Japanese office in Peking, returning to their posts after completing their tour of duty.

Memorandum Trade became the barometer of political relations between Japan and the People's Republic and it was a useful instrument through which the Chinese could exercise pressure on the pro-PRC elements within the LDP and in business circles. Because of the difficulties of the political relationship, the volume of exchanges under it was small when compared with that under 'Friendly Trade' (see Table II, below). In 1971 'Friendly Trade' accounted for 91 per cent of the Japan-China trade, compared with 9 per cent handled through Memorandum Trade.

Political Issues

The political climate between Tokyo and Peking remained turbulent until Kishi was forced out of office by the national convulsions over the revision of the Security Treaty with the United States.[40] The next Prime Minister, Ikeda Hayato, professed a positive attitude towards relations with the People's Republic of China and its eventual recognition.[41] Notwithstanding his moderate and deliberately low-key foreign policy, relations with Peking began to deteriorate towards the end of his term in office. In fact, the Japanese passed through two crises in their relations with Taipei and Peking. The first was at the end of 1963 and the beginning of 1964, the second occurred in mid-1965 and marked the end of the second cycle.

The government had indicated its readiness in principle to authorize deferred payments through the Export-Import Bank for the sale of steel and fertilizers to mainland China. In August 1963 it approved a five-year deferred payment plan whereby the Kurashiki Rayon Company would sell a vinylon plant to China. A request from Taipei that the approval should be withheld was rejected. The Nationalist Chinese threatened reprisals and called on other countries to join in forcing Japan to suspend its 'aid' to the Communist régime. Just as the Japanese were trying to mend fences with Taipei, a new incident took place. A member of a visiting technical mission from Communist China, Chou Hung-ching by name, presented himself at the Russian Embassy in Tokyo on 7 October 1963 and asked for political asylum in the USSR. Later he was reported to have changed his mind and wanted to stay in Japan or go to Taiwan. In November he apparently changed his mind once more and expressed a wish to return to China, to which he was repatriated in early 1964. The Nationalist government reacted vigorously, accusing the Japanese of forcing Chou to return to the Mainland. It suspended all new procurements from Japan and almost broke off diplomatic relations. This led the Japanese to send ex-Prime Minister Yoshida to Taipei in February 1964 to soothe the irate Nationalists and to deal with the vexed question of trade with the Mainland.

After his return from Taipei, Yoshida wrote to Chiang's Chief Secretary, saying that, at least for the remainder of the year, the Japanese government would not allow industrial plants to be exported to China with the assistance of official credit facilities. In the summer Foreign Minister Ōhira Masayoshi visited Taipei and relations with the Nationalist government returned to normal.

Although the government had begun to refuse export credits in the last months of the Ikeda administration, Peking reserved its bitterest hostility for his successor, Satō Eisaku, Kishi's younger brother, who became Premier on 9 November 1964. In the first half of 1965 Peking cancelled a whole series of contracts with Japanese firms, ostensibly because of the government's unfriendly attitude and because it allowed the Kuomintang to interfere with Sino-Japanese trade.

Satō's relationship to Kishi and the record of his administration suggest that official Japanese policy once again veered strongly towards Taiwan and the American position over the China problem. But this is not an accurate picture either of Satō's position or that of the Japanese government. Six months before taking office, Satō had made substantial promises about improvements in Sino-Japanese relations to Nan Han-chen, who was visiting the Communist Chinese trade fair in Japan in his capacity as chairman of the China International Trade Promotion Committee. Satō expressed his determination to break the deadlock in Sino-Japanese relations if he came to power, and described the policy of separating politics from economics as the proverbial folly of 'scratching the itchy foot over the shoe'.[42]

At an even earlier time Satō had criticized Ikeda's cautious foreign policy and had insisted that the restoration of diplomatic relations with China was an urgent and important task for Japan. A member of his faction in the LDP had described him as a 'Japanese de Gaulle' and had forecast dramatic action once he was in power – an interesting comparison because it tells us something about the prestige in Japan of the man who was following an independent foreign policy within the context of an alliance with the United States.

On assuming office, Satō seemed to be living up to his promises and to the expectations held of him. He went to Washington for talks with President Johnson. They revealed some differences in their perspectives on China. The Americans, now deeply involved in Vietnam, were markedly more hostile towards the People's Republic than were the

Japanese and Mr Satō emphasized Japan's determination to pursue its own policy towards Peking.

However, another Satō had emerged immediately on his investiture, who gave good reason for Peking's mistrust. His first speech to the Diet as Premier included a declaration to the effect that he would follow a policy of separating politics from economics when dealing with China. The two faces of Satō's policy towards China, which were to distinguish official policy throughout his administration, the longest in Japan's postwar history, are not to be taken merely as proof of his devious personality, but illustrated, perhaps more clearly than at any other time, the dilemmas of Japanese policy. The reasons for these tergiversations will be considered in the next chapter.

CYCLE III : 1965–1971

The International Background
The international background of the third cycle in Japan's relations with China was one of conflict and accommodation. The United States was deeply involved in the Vietnam War throughout the period, adding new strains to the American-Japanese relationship. The strains were not confined to growing Japanese opposition to the conflict and fears of being drawn into it, but also stemmed from the economic consequences of the war for both countries. The Japanese, as in the earlier Korean War, were the beneficiaries of the huge American expenditures, with the consequence that the turn of the decade saw a serious balance of payments problem emerging between the two countries.

From the middle of 1969 onwards there was a marked trend in American policy which pointed towards an eventual accommodation with China (see Appendix E, below). In the same year there emerged unmistakable signs that after the turmoil of the Cultural Revolution, China was becoming more actively involved in international politics. The China which thus emerged from a few years of almost complete isolation had become a nuclear-armed China, the first test explosion having taken place in 1964. One obvious reason for China's renewed international activities was the perceived need to counter Russian influence, for the Sino-Soviet conflict had reached new heights of intensity with border clashes on the Ussuri river in 1969. The Soviet Union was gradually replacing the United States in Chinese eyes as enemy number one.

Trade Relations
The developments under this rubric can be described very briefly. The impact of the Cultural Revolution on the Chinese economy was not

nearly so devastating as appeared at first sight. Sino-Japanese trade, which had been increasing rapidly in value since 1964, did not fall off on anything like the scale that it did after 1958, and began to pick up again quite substantially after 1969 (see Table I, below). However, although trade with China was increasing in value, its proportion to Japan's total foreign trade hardly changed at all. In fact, it declined somewhat from near to 3 per cent in the early years of this cycle to about 2 per cent in the later years.

Commercial relations became more and more intertwined with the political issues between the two countries. When the L-T Trade Agreement expired at the end of 1967 the Chinese renewed it only on an annual basis. From then on the annual negotiations for renewal became long-drawn-out affairs, with the Chinese insisting on a communiqué which explicitly accepted their view of relations with Japan, and the Japanese, under heavy pressure from the authorities at home, trying to tone it down. In the end they invariably accepted the Chinese position more or less willingly.

Political Issues
Satō had become totally unacceptable to Peking. He had visited Chiang Kai-shek in September 1967. When Chiang's son, Chiang Ching-kuo, paid a return visit to Tokyo in November, the Chinese Communists vigorously denounced Satō's conspiracy with the United States and the Soviet Union 'to set foot on the sacred soil of China'. The China question had, however, become an issue of great importance in Japanese politics; an issue that was accentuated by sharp divisions within the LDP.

Even within the cabinet there were different views on China policy. We catch a glimpse of this at a cabinet meeting held on 19 September 1966, when the Foreign Minister said that he would take the American line over Chinese representation in the UN. On the other hand, the Director-General of the Economic Planning Agency argued against co-sponsorship of the American resolution and for a more independent position over the issue.[43]

Towards the end of the decade there were some signs that Japan was seeking to establish official relations with the People's Republic. This drift in Japanese policy became apparent about a year before a corresponding change became noticeable in American policy.

The Foreign Ministry announced on 24 April 1968 that since the beginning of the year unofficial contacts had taken place between Japanese and Chinese diplomats in Norway, Holland, Switzerland, and Laos. Sixteen days after a warning from Chiang Kai-shek about the dangerous consequences of Japanese moves towards the People's Republic, Deputy Foreign Minister Kurauchi revealed on 24 June that he had informed the Chinese through various diplomatic missions that Japan was ready for talks about steps to improve relations.

None the less, Japanese policy remained ambiguous. For instance, in early 1969 the Prime Minister said that Japan did not favour a two Chinas policy and followed a different line from that of the United States. Yet, he also insisted that the 'Government regards Nationalist China as the sole legitimate Government of China.'[44] Another much remarked upon ambiguity occurred during Mr Satō's visit to Washington in November 1969 for talks with President Nixon. The terms of the communiqué that was issued after their meetings referred to Japan's concern over the security of the Republic of Korea and of Taiwan, but there was a subtle distinction in the wording. It stated that the 'security of the Republic of Korea was essential to Japan's own security,' whereas 'security in the Taiwan area' was mentioned as 'also a most important factor for the security of Japan'.[45] Some observers interpreted this to mean that Japan reserved its position over Taiwan, giving less assurance that it would automatically support the United States in a conflict in that area.

Although the equivocal approach in public statements on the China question continued right up to the announcement of President Nixon's trip to Peking, there could be little doubt on the general direction of Japanese policy. For, on 22 January 1971 Satō for the first time referred to the *People's Republic of China* in a policy speech before the Diet. Another shift in Japanese policy had been indicated some weeks earlier when Foreign Minister Aichi announced that at the next session of the General Assembly of the United Nations, in the autumn of 1971, Japan would not co-sponsor the resolution designating the issue of Chinese representation as an important question, requiring a two-thirds majority of the members present and voting – a procedural device by which Peking had been prevented from occupying China's seat.

NOTES

1   In the summer of 1976 the Japanese Ministry of Foreign Affairs declassified approximately one hundred thousand pages of documents covering the period of the Occupation. The material represents about 10 per cent of all the official records of that time. I have not been able to consult it in preparation for this study.

2   Joseph H. Boyle, *China and Japan at War 1937–1945: the Politics of Collaboration* (Stanford, Calif., Stanford UP, 1972), pp. 167–74, 187–92.

3   For example, Shigemitsu Mamoru (Minister to China in 1934) and Matsumoto Shigeharu (one of Prince Konoe's closest advisers) both had influential roles in postwar Japan. Saionji Kinkazu (grandson of Prince

Saionji and another of Konoe's confidants) has been tireless in the pursuit of better relations with the People's Republic of China. In 1958 he went to live in Peking and became influential in setting up what later came to be known as Memorandum Trade. Ibid., pp. 34, 140–1, 177–8, 181–2, 186, 307.

4 Round-table interview with Kanō Hisaakira, Major-General Watanabe Wataru, and Baron Ijūin Toraichi, 3 Oct 1945, reported in *New York Herald Tribune*, 9 Oct 1945. Boyle, pp. 64–5, 102–3.

5 *New York Herald Tribune*, 18 and 24 Sep 1945; *North China Daily News*, 19 June 1948; *Christian Science Monitor*, 23 Dec 1948.

6 Boyle, pp. 326–31; *North China Daily News*, 1 Feb 1949; *The Times*, 4 May 1949.

7 This tradition goes back to the Tokugawa period. See Tsunoda Ryūsaku, Theodore de Bary, and Donald Keene, eds., *Sources of Japanese Tradition*, vol. II (New York, Columbia UP, 1964), pp. 70–3; Boyle, pp. 345–6; Delmer M. Brown, *Nationalism in Japan: an Introductory Historical Analysis* (Berkeley, Univ. of California Press, 1955), p. 68.

8 *New York Herald Tribune*, 18 and 24 Sep 1945.

9 Trade with the Mainland as percentages of Japan's total imports and exports:

Year	Imports	Exports
1946	1·6	4·6
1947	1·0	5·9
1948	3·6	1·6
1949	2·4	0·6
1950	4·0	2·4
1951	1·1	0·4
1952	0·7	0·1

Source: Abstracted from Fukui Haruhiro, *Party in Power: the Japanese Liberal-Democrats and Policy-Making* (Berkeley, Univ. of California Press, 1970), p. 229, Table 25.

10 George P. Jan, 'Japan's Trade with Communist China', *Asian Survey*, vol. IX, no. 12, Dec 1969, p. 904, Table 2.

11 *North China Daily News*, 10 and 31 Dec 1947, 16 Jan 1948.

12 Ibid., 27 Apr 1948.

13 Ibid., 21 July 1948.

14 Broadcast on 15 Aug 1945. *News Chronicle*, 16 Aug 1945.

15 For a discussion of Nationalist Chinese policy towards Japan under the Occupation, see Gordon Daniels, 'Nationalist China in the Allied Council; Policies towards Japan, 1946–52', *The Hokkaido Law Review*, vol. XXVII, no. 2, Nov 1976, pp. 165–88. See also, *New York Times*, 2 Nov 1946; *North China Daily News*, 2 Aug 1947.

16 *North China Daily News*, 14 Apr and 4 May 1949; *South China Morning Post*, 4 and 8 June 1949; *Christian Science Monitor*, 9 June 1949; *New York Times*, 25 Nov 1949.

17 *New York Times*, 4 Feb 1950.

18   Trade with Taiwan as percentages of Japan's total imports and exports:

Year	Imports	Exports
1946	0·7	0·04
1947	0·3	0·3
1948	1·0	0·01
1949	3·1	1·6
1950	3·7	4·5
1951	2·5	3·7
1952	3·1	4·7

Source: Fukui, p. 229, Table 25.

19   See Dean Acheson's note to the UN Secretary-General, 21 Sep 1950. Margaret Carlyle, ed., *Documents on International Affairs 1949–50* (London, OUP for RIIA, 1953), pp. 665–7. This should be compared with the earlier statements of President Truman and Secretary of State Acheson, made on 5 Jan 1950, in which they emphasized Chinese sovereignty over the island. *The Department of State Bulletin*, vol. XXII, no. 550, 16 Jan 1950, pp. 79–81. On the other hand, it has been asserted that '. . . the United States has never failed to recognize the existence of a nation formerly called China of which Taiwan formed an integral part. . . .' Bernard Brodie, *War and Politics* (London, Cassell, 1974), p. 109, n. 41.

20   Denise Folliot, ed., *Documents on International Affairs 1951* (London, OUP for RIIA, 1954), p. 612.

21   *Survey of International Affairs 1939–46*: F. C. Jones and others, *The Far East 1942–1946* (London, OUP for RIIA, 1955), p. 491.

22   *The Department of State Bulletin*, vol. XIII, no. 318, 29 July 1945, p. 137.

23   *New York Times*, 14 Sep 1951.

24   This refers to the General Assembly Resolution 498(V), 1 Feb 1951, which described the Chinese intervention in the Korean War as an act of aggression. Dusan J. Djonovich, ed., *United Nations Resolutions*: Series I, *Resolutions Adopted by the General Assembly*, vol. III, 1950–1952 (Dobbs Ferry, NY, Oceana Publications, 1973), p. 159.

25   For a discussion of the 'Yoshida Letter' and American opinion, see Bernard C. Cohen, *The Political Process and Foreign Policy: the Making of the Japanese Peace Settlement* (Princeton, NJ, Princeton UP, 1957), pp. 150–4.

26   *Nippon Times*, 23 May 1952.

27   After the signature of the Treaty with the Republic of China, Wajima Eiji, Director of the Gaimushō's Asia Bureau, implied in the Diet that Japan had recognized the Nationalist government as the government of the Mainland. This interpretation was corrected almost immediately by the head of the Ministry's Information and Cultural Affairs Section. *New York Times*, 22 June 1952.

28   Dai Ichiji Nicchū Bōeki Kyōtei [First Japan-China Trade Pact], 1 June 1952, reproduced in Ishikawa T. and others, eds., *Sengo Shiryō: Nicchū Kankei* (Tokyo, Nihon Hyōron-sha, 1970), pp. 23–4.

29 In addition to the items under the COCOM list, which had been set up to cover trade with the Soviet Union and East Europe, CHINCOM included 200 further items. Japan promised the US to apply even stricter controls on its trade with mainland China than those exercised by the West European countries. The exchange restrictions imposed by the US on the use of dollars for transactions with China and North Korea were another serious impediment for Japan. Shao-chuan Leng, *Japan and Communist China* (Kyoto, Dōshisha UP, 1958), pp. 43–5, 47–8.

30 The Chinese imposed a counter-embargo in response to that of the West. They divided their export and import commodities into three classes under this system. The classification was designed to match certain types of Chinese exports with certain types of imports. Thus, Class A exports could be exchanged only for Class A imports. Class B exports could be exchanged only for Class A and B imports. Class C exports could be traded for A, B, or C imports. This created difficulties for the Japanese. For instance, Chinese Class A exports included iron ore, coal, and soybeans, items most sought after by the Japanese, and could be exchanged only for Class A imports from Japan, which happened to be items subject to the Western embargo. It is, therefore, not surprising that trade languished. Ibid., pp. 45–6, 69, n. 9.

31 Percentage fulfilments under the first three agreements were as follows:

Agreement	Exports	Imports
(1) June 1952 to Oct 1953	4	6
(2) Oct 1953 to Dec 1954	27·7	41
(3) May 1955 to May 1956	36·7	91·3

Ibid. See also Fukui, p. 228.

32 Hatoyama Shushō no Hatsukakugigo no Kisha Kaiken ni okeru Hatsugen [Prime Minister Hatoyama's press conference after his first cabinet meeting], 10 Dec 1954: see Ishikawa and others, eds., *Sengo Shiryō: Nicchū Kankei*, p. 46.

33 Leng, p. 14. For further information about Hatoyama's attitude to relations with China, see Fukui, pp. 230, 238.

34 Uchida Kenzō, *Sengo Nihon no Hoshu Seiji* (Tokyo, Iwanami Shoten, 1969), p. 186. For Kishi's attitudes towards China, see Fukui, ch. 9. There is also an interesting if somewhat journalistic biography by Dan Kurzman, *Kishi and Japan: the Search for the Sun* (New York, Ivan Obolensky, 1960). It contains some biographical information not usually found in more academic books. See especially pp. 298, 370–2.

35 Doi Akira, 'Two Years' Exchanges with China', *Japan Quarterly*, vol. V, no. 4, Oct–Dec 1958, pp. 435–51. This is a useful chronological account of events during the first one and a half years of Kishi's premiership, concentrating particularly on the evolution of Chinese policy. It is also noteworthy that the Japanese government conferred closely with the Chinese Nationalists before making clear its position over the status of the trade missions. (Ibid., p. 410.)

36 Ibid., pp. 402–3. A useful summary of the Sino-Soviet dispute is to be found in A. Doak Barnett, *Uncertain Passage: China's Transition to*

the Post-Mao Era (Washington, The Brookings Institution, 1974), pp. 259–65.

37 *Japan Quarterly*, vol. X, no. 2, Apr–June 1963, pp. 145–7.

38 Uchida, p. 192.

39 Memorandum Trade was distinguished in several ways. It was organized under periodic agreements, the original agreement was for five years and expired in Dec 1967. Each agreement fixed the items and volume to be traded under its terms. The procedure was supervised by the Japan-China Overall Trade Liaison Consultation Council, representing the associations of manufacturers dealing with the items. For example, if a manufacturer of machines wanted to trade under the scheme, he had first to join the industrial association of those who made his type of machine, such as the Machine Tool Industry Association or the Textile Machine Industry Association. The association was affiliated to the Japan-China Machine Tools Trade Consultation Council, which, in turn, was a member of the Japan-China Overall Trade Liaison Consultation Council.

In order to have 'Friendly Trade' it was necessary to join a 'friendly' organization, such as the Japan-China Friendship Association or the Japan International Trade Promotion Association (Kokubōsoku). Firms had to subscribe to the three political principles enunciated by the Chinese in Aug 1958 and had to be recognized by the Chinese as 'friendly'. By the end of Mar 1971, 345 firms were listed as 'friendly'. Some of Japan's largest trading houses were engaged in the China trade through dummy companies, thus enabling them to do business with Taiwan as well.

In effect, all firms trading with the Mainland, whether through Memorandum Trade or 'Friendly Trade', had to be acceptable to the Chinese. In the case of the former, the Japanese nominated them, but this was not done without prior agreement from the Chinese. In the case of the latter, the onus of approval was on the Chinese. Hence, most of the firms trading under the MT system were designated as 'Friendly'.

A useful summary of Memorandum and 'Friendly' trade is to be found in Japan External Trade Organization (JETRO), *How to Approach the China Market* (Tokyo, Press International, 1972), ch. V, 'Reopening of Japan-China Trade', pp. 75–82. The book also includes detailed descriptions of the mechanics of the trade, as well as most of the important documents relating to it. Other sources include *The Current Situation and Problems of Japan-China Trade* (Tokyo, Bank of Japan, Research Bureau, 27 Aug 1971), 14–16; Suga E., Yamamoto T., and Shiranishi S., *Nicchū Mondai-Gendai Chūgoku to Kōryū no Shikaku* (Tokyo, Hanseidō, 1971), pp. 271–5; Yasui A., 'Nicchū Bōeki no Shōrai to Sangyō-kai', *Keizai Hyōron*, Jan 1971, p. 150.

40 A very thorough account of the crisis in 1960 is given in George R. Packard, *Protest in Tokyo: the Security Treaty Crisis of 1960* (Princeton, NJ, Princeton UP, 1966).

41 Uchida, pp. 194–5.

42 *JT*, 19 Aug 1972.

43 *Japan Quarterly*, vol. XIV, no. 1, Jan–Mar 1967, p. 117.

44 *JT*, 6 Mar 1969. See also Foreign Minister Aichi's statement in the Diet on 15 Mar 1971, that concepts of 'pre-war' international law about 'one government in one nation' did not apply to the China problem. He thereby indicated a two Chinas or one China/one Taiwan formula as a solution. (*Japan Quarterly*, vol. XVIII, no. 3, July–Sep 1971, p. 359.)

45 The relevant passage in the communiqué of 21 Nov 1969 is as follows: 'The Prime Minister deeply appreciated the peacekeeping efforts of the United Nations in the area and stated that the security of the Republic of Korea was essential to Japan's own security. The President and the Prime Minister shared the hope that Communist China would adopt a more cooperative and constructive attitude in its external relations. The President referred to the treaty obligations of his country to the Republic of China which the United States would uphold. The Prime Minister said that the maintenance of peace and security in the Taiwan area was also a most important factor for the security of Japan.' (*The Department of State Bulletin*, vol. LXI, no. 1590, 15 Dec 1969, p. 555.)

2 China Issues after Twenty Years: 1971

THE three cyclical periods in Sino-Japanese relations after 1952 have a certain similarity at first sight. Each began at a time when relations between mainland China and Japan were minimal and the Chinese Communists were expressing hostility towards the government in Tokyo. As the years passed, contacts picked up again and developed new forms. Things then moved to a fresh climax in which the various channels of communication were all but blocked for a relatively short period.

A quick reading of the events suggests that the zigzag course of Japanese policy was largely dictated by two factors. The first includes all the external stimuli: the initiatives and pressures from mainland China, and the countervailing initiatives and pressures from Taiwan and the United States. The second includes all the domestic pressures: the interests and biases of businessmen, politicians, and bureaucrats. The formal and informal ties to Taiwan and the United States, as well as the political power of the pro-Kuomintang lobby in Japan, were strong enough to create periodic breakdowns in relations with the Mainland. Nevertheless, the attraction of China was sufficiently compelling to produce ceaseless attempts at establishing new forms of relationship. Even if the generally pro-Kuomintang governments in Tokyo did not countenance these efforts officially, they usually turned a blind eye to them and at times encouraged them.

The response to the China problem during the different cycles was not the same and we can detect changes in attitudes and policy as Japanese perspectives on China and the international situation changed. Yet a glance at the history of the twenty years after 1952 suggests that the main issues, which had emerged by the end of the Occupation, remain useful analytical categories for a discussion of Japanese policy on the eve of the events which transformed Japan's postwar relations with China.

Such a bald statement raises a number of further questions. What explains the continuing importance of the issues throughout the period? To what extent had each retained its signficance? Or did the impact of some lessen while others increased in importance? How far were the problems surrounding each major issue more or less the same in 1971 as in 1952, or how far were they transformed by developments within Japan and abroad? Finally, did completely new issues emerge during this period? I will attempt to address these questions by looking at each of the issues in turn.

TRADE

Trade continued to be the most important material issue between the two countries throughout the twenty years. It reflected the state of relations with the PRC. When they were relaxed, there was a steadily increasing flow; when they were strained, the tap was almost turned off. To a large extent it was China that dictated how much trade there should be, not only out of political considerations but also in response to the development and needs of its economy. Japan was further restrained by the pressures which came from the United States and Taiwan, and the conflicting pulls of the Taiwan and mainland lobbies at home. Commerce was, therefore, the barometer of the political climate between Japan and China. After all, there was little else it could be measured by. The exchange of persons (see Table III, below) was minimal when one takes account of the size of their populations, although it is true that those who went to China had an influence on public opinion far beyond their small numbers. The many official statements of the leaders of both countries have an uneven utility. A careful reading of Chinese utterances can throw some light on the shifts of Chinese policy. The utterances of Japanese ministers and officials are far less useful guides to policy. The actual amount of trade was small, even in the best years, particularly when compared with the large volume of trade before the war. The reasons for this state of affairs are to be found in the evolution of both economies during the two decades.

The founders of Chinese communism had taken note of the lessons of the past. They learnt how easy it is for a country with a backward economy to fall under the control of foreign powers in its attempt to modernize through the introduction of foreign capital and technology. They saw one solution to the problem of modernization in the experience of Meiji Japan, where the process was carried out through the acquisition of foreign technology without much direct investment of foreign capital. They must have been deeply impressed to observe how the Japanese leaders of the nineteenth century were able to keep a tight grip over the national economy in spite of revolutionary changes in its structure through the large-scale adoption of Western knowledge and methods.

None the less, they could not emulate the Japanese example after 1949. The environment of the mid-twentieth was different from that of the late nineteenth century. The Chinese revolution had taken place as a result of a long struggle against a strongly entrenched foreign imperialism, unlike the Japanese revolution, which stemmed from a deliberate decision to forestall the threat of foreign domination. Above all, the development of the Japanese economy and social institutions before the Meiji Restoration had laid the foundation for the rapid construction of a modern industrial state. The Chinese economy and social institutions, on the other hand, were ill adapted to meet the challenge from outside. Thus, the ultimate Chinese revolution was conceived in a different ideological dimension.

The Chinese adopted the principles of Western socialism according to Marxist theory, with important modifications to suit the Chinese context. The application of these principles to relationships with other countries was alleged to require that foreign aid be secondary to self-help, and that, as far as possible, all relations should be reciprocal. Thus, China had to avoid becoming dependent on long-term credits, should not allow foreign investment, and must be in a position to pay for all purchases.

While this may be taken as a summary of China's basic policy in the 1960s – although the Chinese were quite happy to accept credits from the Japanese Export-Import Bank in 1963–4 – it has to be remembered that the principles were to a large extent a rationalization stemming from the condition and problems of the Chinese economy as well as from China's unfortunate experiences with the Soviet Union.

In the reconstruction of China's economy during the early 1950s the industrial sector was given priority over agriculture. This policy had been accompanied by a rapid expansion of foreign trade, which was reflected in the increasing volume of exchanges with Japan. But that was small beer compared with the extent of China's economic relationship with the Soviet Union.

In 1949 the Chinese believed that they would become members of a new community of socialist states. In those early years they were quite ready to accept the Soviet model to some extent. This, combined with a material dependence on Russia, was not so repugnant to Mao as he claimed later. China's rulers probably did not imagine that economic imperialism could be a feature of the relationship between two socialist states. Their experience with the Russians undoubtedly strengthened their belief in self-sufficiency and their suspicion of foreign economic entanglements.

The Great Leap Forward of 1958 and the new emphasis on the agricultural sector may have been a part consequence of the break with the Soviet Union, but the disastrous consequences of these policies caused a general decline in foreign trade, so that the reduction in commerce with Japan (see Table I, below) must be attributed to economic as well as political factors.

The rapid increase in the volume of bilateral trade in 1964 and 1965 reflects a recovery in the Chinese economy. It also indicates that China had now become dependent on the industrialized countries of the Western world for its machinery and technology. This gave Japan a great advantage, as can be seen from its growing importance among China's trading partners, but at the same time it created a serious balance of payments problem which affected the Sino-Japanese political relationship over the issue of deferred payments.

While the size of the country and its resources, the condition of the national economy (in which agriculture was the pivotal sector), historical experience, and the philosophy of Mao all favoured China's policy of self-sufficiency and small reliance on foreign trade, the opposite was true of Japan. Since the war there has been a fundamental shift in the national economy and in the pattern of external trade.[1] The postwar growth of the Japanese economy was not led by foreign trade. Instead, domestic investment provided the greatest stimulus. Japan is, however, almost wholly dependent on imports for sources of energy and the supply of many raw materials. With the exception of the United States, which supplied large quantities of food and coal, they came mainly from countries which were underdeveloped or had small populations. This resulted in substantial imbalances of payments with those countries, except again the United States, because they could not absorb a sufficient proportion of Japanese goods in return. Japan compensated for the deficit by exporting to industrialized countries with large markets, particularly the United States and western Europe, thereby running up large surpluses in its trading account with them.

From the early 1960s onwards the average annual growth rate of the Japanese economy jumped from around 5 to 11 per cent. In the course of expansion severe constraints appeared which influenced the direction of economic growth. Increasing labour costs, higher educational levels and the resulting difficulties of filling jobs at the 'lower end' of the economy, coupled with the high cost of living and environmental problems, caused the decline of some labour-intensive industries and their 'export' to neighbouring countries where cheap trained manpower was available, notably South Korea, Taiwan, and some states in Southeast Asia. The movement of industries abroad was not wholly welcome in the countries of Southeast Asia, where it was seen as part of a new Japanese imperialism.

Within Japan there was a steady advance into the fields of heavy industry (shipbuilding, car manufacturing, steel, chemicals, etc.) and high technology and so-called knowledge-intensive industries (electronics, communications), which placed it in the first rank of the developed countries. Outside Japan there was increasing investment in the extraction of raw materials and sources of energy, notably oil and natural gas, as well as in some manufacturing industries. As with reparations after the war, these efforts served to strengthen the Japanese economy and benefited the host countries only incidentally.

While investment was concentrated heavily, though not exclusively, in the resource-rich countries of Southeast Asia, and, more recently, in the oil-producing states of the Middle East, the general pattern of trade shifted substantially towards the industrialized countries. Between one-quarter and one-third of Japan's foreign trade was with the United States alone.

The postwar economic development of Japan and of the international environment, in which the economic policies of the communist countries have played their part, completely reversed the importance of China to the Japanese economy. Nevertheless, Japan retained a very strong interest in the potential for economic relations with China.

The 'lure' of the China market, a mixture of nostalgia and need, became a constant feature in Japanese attitudes towards China. Early in 1965, former Premier Yoshida wrote that, without solving the China problem, there was no way to solve the problems of Asia. Japan could attain prosperity only through tapping the Chinese market with its population of seven hundred million. The trends of that market provided the key to the problems of Asia and were a matter of life and death for Japan's industries.[2]

Yoshida was going against the advice of economists who had warned ever since 1949 against placing exaggerated importance on China in Japan's economic strategy. The interest and fascination of the China market none the less continued unabated. They were fanned by the Chinese and their friends in Japan for political purposes and were strengthened from time to time by the need for new outlets, either because outlets elsewhere had been closed or because of excess production at home. In 1962, for instance, the chemical fertilizer industry was not very interested in the Chinese market. Ten years later, as a result of over-production, it was spearheading the campaign to enter it.

Although the evidence from the economic development of both countries pointed strongly against any but rather small benefits to be derived from the China trade, it did not quite answer the objections of those who maintained that the evidence was the consequence of Japan's unfriendly attitude towards China. If Japanese governments had refused to be associated with American policies, had accepted Peking's position over Taiwan, and had accepted the offers of 'normal' relationships made by Chinese leaders at various times, then the 'evidence' might very well have been different. In theory, both China and Japan should have benefited from close association : the Chinese would have had access to a very advanced technology, to investment capital, and would have enjoyed the benefits coming from geographical proximity; the Japanese would have gained from having a market so close at hand, especially if they could tap the substantial resources of their neighbours.

No doubt, this was at the back of Yoshida's mind in 1965 and influencing many others who wrote and spoke of the promise of Sino-Japanese relations. Moreover, quite substantial economic interests were behind all those who longed for more trade and economic collaboration with China. Before considering the political and other obstacles in the way of such policies, we must examine the political weight of these special economic interests in the policy-making process.

The phenomenal economic growth combined with the low profile of Japan in international politics naturally drew a great deal of attention to economic interests, which, it was assumed, dominated national policy in the 1960s. Because of the nature of big business and its control of large sectors of the national economy, the role of *zaikai** in the policy-making process has been closely scrutinized in the past twenty years. More recent studies have revealed that this approach, based on size and wealth, is misleading and that it is necessary to analyse economic interests vertically as well as horizontally.

Japanese business organization may be observed at three levels : the individual firm (*kigyō*); the *gyōkai*,[3] associations of particular industrial interests such as steelmaking, textiles, agriculture, fisheries, etc.; the *zaikai*. The *gyōkai* are often the most significant in terms of political impact. The textile industry is a good example. It is concentrated in certain parts of the country and has an important influence on voting in some constituencies. The workers are organized in company unions and they and their families can be mobilized at election time, which is of more help to candidates than money. The individual firm, on the other hand, is generally too weak to play a significant part in politics and the importance of *zaikai* in influencing decisions has been exaggerated. The fact that big business was the paymaster of the Liberal-Democratic Party and that the heads of major concerns often had direct links with the leaders of particular factions in the Party had the paradoxical effect of weakening its overall influence. Business leaders were apt to speak with different voices on key issues.

* *Zaikai* is a term which has been used to refer to 'business circles', 'financial circles', 'business community', and even 'leaders of big business'. I have used it to mean 'big business', i.e. the large commercial banks, the giant trading houses like C. Itoh, Marubeni, Mitsui, Nisshō-Iwai, the major industrial corporations, like Shin Nippon Steel, Sanyō, Hitachi, Tokyo Shibaura Electric Co. (Tōshiba), Matsushita Electric, Toyota, Nissan, etc.

The Federation of Economic Organizations (FEO) – Keidanren – the supreme co-ordinating body of big business, whose president is regarded as 'prime minister' of *zaikai*'s 'invisible government', favoured the *status quo* of formal relations with Taipei and making the best of informal contacts with the Mainland, provided they did not upset political relationships with the United States and the Nationalist Republic of China. The Japan Chamber of Commerce and Industry (Nisshō) was, broadly speaking, in the same camp, although it served as spokesman for small and medium-sized enterprises, many of which were attracted to the China trade and were themselves the special target of Chinese propaganda. Moreover, in the early years after 1952 it had been dominated by Fujiyama Aiichirō, one of the leaders of the pro-PRC lobby in the LDP during the 1960s.

The pro-Peking elements included many businesses in Kansai, and individual industrialists such as Kawai Yoshinari, President of the Komatsu Manufacturing Company, and Matsubara Yosomatsu of the Hitachi Shipbuilding Company. However, as an example of how difficult it is to divide business leaders into clearly defined pro-Peking and pro-Taipei camps, it is worth noting that Kawai was one of the group of businessmen who had supported Kishi; a group which also included Adachi Tadashi, an ardent partisan of the Nationalist Republic of China.

During the crisis of 1960 the pro-China elements, concentrated in the textile industry, were anti-Treaty. The Japan Federation of Employers' Associations (Nikkeiren), on the other hand, took a hard pro-Kishi, pro-Treaty line. The Japan Committee for Economic Development (JCED) assumed a middle-of-the-road position and supported the faction of Miki Takeo who, in later years, became a leading advocate of improved relations with China.

Big business has never been fully integrated into the process of foreign-policy making. It represents a diversity of interests which, as can be seen over trade with China, leads to very different approaches on any issue. Even when one of the major economic organizations makes a public statement over policy, prominent businessmen often contradict it. Business leaders hold conflicting political opinions and they have different political friendships.

When basic economic policy is at stake the national leadership of industry works closely with the bureaucrats of the General Affairs Department in the Ministry of International Trade and Industry. On specific issues which involve important political considerations, such as relations with China, its influence is marginal for several reasons. Interest in China has been very uneven and those firms and *gyōkai* which favoured closer relations have exercised pressure through the appropriate bureau of MITI, through links with Diet members, and through public opinion. Their importance should not be underestimated, but the great majority of the business community would not have sacrificed relations with the US for the sake of improved trade with China.

TAIWAN

A comparison between Japan's trade with Taiwan and Japan's trade with the Mainland during the two decades under review reveals a see-saw effect (see Tables I and IV, below). Between 1952 and 1955 the Taiwan trade was ahead on all counts. By 1956 it was behind in total value, although ahead in exports. Between 1958 and 1962 it was ahead again in all respects. The pattern was reversed between 1964 and 1966, when the trade with Taiwan fell behind in everything – to a very considerable extent in 1966. From then onwards, until 1972, Japanese exports to Taiwan surged ahead, while the value of imports lagged behind that of imports from the Mainland (they were almost equal in 1970). Because of the rapid increase of the value of exports to Taiwan, the overall value of trade with it was greater and the gap seemed to widen in these last few years.

Despite the fluctuations, the differences in the amount of trade between Japan and the two countries are only marginal. For Japan, the volume of its trade with each was only a small percentage of its rapidly burgeoning foreign trade. The reverse was not true of Taiwan, whose Japan trade was a considerable percentage of its foreign trade, nor was it true of mainland China, where trade with Japan took a rapidly increasing share of foreign trade from 1965 onwards. Japanese trade with Taiwan usually surged ahead of trade with China during the years when relations with Peking were particularly strained, that is, at the beginning of the first cycle, in the period between 1958 and 1962, and again in the last years of the third cycle. During years of détente, such as the middle 1950s and the middle 1960s, trade with the Mainland assumed greater importance. This feature strengthened those who wanted more trade with China to press harder for the normalization of relations.

The balance of trade with both countries tended to favour Japan. In the early 1950s imports and exports were more or less in balance in the Taiwan trade, from then on exports were ahead, except in 1963 and 1964. Trade with the Mainland followed a different pattern, with imports in excess of exports and a turnabout in the proportion after 1964, although the gap did not become as great as in the trade with Taiwan during the last years of the third cycle.

One feature which was absent from Japan's economic relations with the People's Republic but had an important bearing on economic relations with Taiwan, was Japanese investment in the economy. It accounted for a quarter of all investments in Taiwan after 1954 and reached a total of US $650 million by the end of September 1972. Japanese technical and licensing agreements also accounted for a high proportion of all such links between Taiwanese business and foreign countries. The ties between overseas Chinese merchants, who played a substantial role in the economies of many Southeast Asian countries, and Taiwan during this period added to Japan's interest in the island. Finally, despite the relatively modest Taiwanese exports to Japan, various trading houses of Tokyo and Ōsaka between them handled about one half of Taiwan's total exports by the beginning of the 1970s.

These last features added an extra dimension to Japanese economic interest in Taiwan and could be said to lend it greater importance than the economic interest in China. Just how significant this 'greater importance' was is another matter. The events of 1971–2, as we shall see, do not suggest that the significance was very great. As for the comparative values of trade with the two countries, our analysis indicates that there was not much to choose between them. Indeed, the rapid forward movement in trade with China in the last three to four years before normalization suggested a very considerable potential for trade with the Mainland in spite of severe economic and political restrictions. The reasons for Taiwan's importance in Japan's China policy must, therefore, be sought in other interests than those which are purely economic.

Taiwan had a symbolic importance in Japanese politics. The associations of prominent politicians of the LDP and various business leaders with the Kuomintang, which had been noticeable under the Occupation and which, in some cases, dated from the pre-war and war years, continued to play their part after 1952. But they were not the only ones. Some postwar leaders, too, had developed personal ties with the Chiang Kai-shek government : they included Yoshida, who was sent to Taipei to mend fences at a delicate moment in Japan's relations with the Republic of China. In his case and that of others one should not ignore a sense of personal obligation which derived from the generally magnanimous attitude displayed towards Japan by the leader of the Kuomintang.

The personal feelings of individual leaders formed part of a more widely held attitude among Japanese people. One may distinguish between two strands in the Japanese view of Taiwan : on the one hand, it was seen as one of the 'two Chinas'; on the other, it was regarded as an entity quite apart from China.

The Japanese did not have the feelings of shame and remorse over their past treatment of Taiwan that they displayed in relation to China, Korea, and some of the countries of Southeast Asia. That is not to say that there was no reason for such emotions. During their fifty years' rule of the island the Japanese were in some respects as ruthless and discriminatory as they were elsewhere in Asia.[4] But when the Chinese occupied Taiwan and the Pescadores after the war, their ruthlessness and discrimination soon made the native Taiwanese look back on the days of Japanese rule with nostalgia; a sentiment which communicated itself to the Japanese.

We, therefore, have to distinguish between sympathy for the Kuomintang and sympathy for the people of Taiwan. The first never commanded the whole-hearted support of the LDP, nor even of all ministers, and it was matched by an animus against the Nationalists among other circles in Japan. The second was more widely shared among the Japanese.

It was not by accident that the first major Taiwanese political leader, Thomas Liao, sought refuge in Japan and there created the Formosa Democratic Independence Party in February 1950. In 1955 he became President of the 'Provisional Government of the Republic of Formosa', which was a failure. Ten years later Liao defected to the Kuomintang. In the meanwhile Taiwanese students in Japan, led by Ong Joktik, a Formosan lecturer at Meiji University, had created the Formosan Association in February 1960 and made some headway, with the help of substantial though clandestine support from the sizeable community of businessmen of Taiwanese origin living in Japan. Opinion polls indicated some support for the Taiwanese independence movement among the Japanese public. However, apart from isolated individuals, like the owner of Radio Kantō, Japanese business interests did not support the political activities of the exiles. In the 1960s the independence movement became active in the United States, where it found a more favourable climate of opinion.[5]

The collaboration between Japanese and Taiwanese (as distinct from mainland Chinese) businessmen on the island was of greater significance from the Japanese point of view. Many Taiwanese firms were financed and controlled by the Japanese. The older generation of Taiwanese felt more at home in a Japanese linguistic and cultural milieu, even though, like other Asians, they complained about the behaviour and practices of Japanese businessmen and visitors in their country.

When the political switch from Taipei to Peking came in 1972, it did not represent a serious break with Japanese sentiments towards Taiwan or in the association between Japanese and Taiwanese businessmen, as it was merely a switch from support of one Chinese group to support for another. The continued *de facto* independence of Taiwan left open the question whether the Japanese might be tempted to support an independent Taiwan. I shall return to this in chapter 5.

The foregoing aspects of Japan's interests and attitudes concerning Taiwan, either individually or taken together, cannot be regarded as constituting insuperable obstacles on the road to normal relations with Peking. At times, as in the summer of 1963, the Japanese authorities ignored or brushed aside protests from Taipei. To be sure, Japan's continued recognition of the Nationalist government was an insuperable obstacle in the eyes of Peking, but the views of Peking are not the main focus of this study.

The main obstacle from the Japanese perspective was the Power that stood behind Taiwan. Some of Taiwan's attempts to curb Japanese trade with China were accompanied by weightier pressures from the United States. During the 1950s the pressure was fairly open; in the 1960s it became more discreet. A few examples must suffice.

After the conclusion of the fourth private China-Japan Trade Agreement in March 1958 the United States Under-Secretary of Commerce, Walter Williams, urged the Japanese to be more cautious in their approach to Peking. When trade talks were resumed with China after the rupture under Kishi, the US Under-Secretary of State, Mr Harriman, warned the Japanese that trade with communist countries would be exploited by them for political purposes. He helped to provoke a reaction in some business and political circles against the trend of the Matsumura-Liao talks which had received the consent of Premier Ikeda. The Prime Minister then resorted to a characteristic Japanese response when the political issues had become too tricky : trade was a matter of private deals over which the government need not take a firm position.

None the less, the Matsumura-Liao talks bore fruit and just before Takasaki Tatsunosuke's visit to Peking in the Autumn of 1962, to sign the Memorandum with Liao Cheng-chih, the American Embassy in Tokyo expressed considerable unease. However, representations were made orally, so that there would be no written evidence which could be used to embarrass American relations with Japan. After all, the crisis over the revision of the Japan-US Security Treaty was still fresh in people's memories.

The reason why American pressures were generally effective is found in the link between the issue of Taiwan and the issue of security. Japan's security was tied to the security of Taiwan through the series of agreements which provided American guarantees to both countries. This fact was acknowledged in the Satō-Nixon communiqué of 1969, although its existence had been implicitly recognized by the Japanese since 1952.

SECURITY

The issue of national security, which seemed so urgent in 1952, continued to exercise Japanese governments throughout the next twenty
years, but the nature of the problem changed. By the 1960s the fears
of a centrally controlled communist threat had lessened, if not vanished.
The spectre of revolution and subversion had momentarily reappeared
in the upheaval over the revision of the Security Treaty in 1960. The
revolutionaries on the university campuses at the end of the decade
professed their admiration for Maoism but probably received no more
than verbal support from China. It is extremely doubtful whether the
authorities saw these disturbances as more than localized nuisances.

The main problem for Japan after 1965 was how to continue to
benefit from the security afforded by the United States without becoming involved in the Vietnam War. The Japanese government had to
avoid too close an identification with the American position in Vietnam,
both for domestic political reasons and the country's wider interests in
the region, which were essentially a matter of free access to the economies of all Southeast Asian countries. Despite generally worded statements of support for the United States, it is unlikely that Japanese
leaders shared the simplified American view of the need to contain
communist aggression (particularly Chinese Communist influence) in
Indochina. They were too close to the mood in Asia not to feel
instinctively that nationalism was a more potent force behind the
Vietnamese movement than the communist ideology.

Nevertheless, if they were not convinced by the picture of an
expansionist China, they still felt uncertain of Chinese intentions
and had no wish to do without the protective mantle of the Seventh
Fleet and American strategic power. Moreover, the reversion of
Okinawa to Japanese administrative control became a major policy
objective in the 1960s. As long as the United States remained in Vietnam and kept its commitments in Asia it was unlikely that reversion
could be obtained without allowing the Americans to retain their
bases on the island and subscribing to basic American policy in Asia.
The mention of Taiwan and of Korea in the Satō-Nixon communiqué
of November 1969, as areas in whose security Japan had a special
interest, was a *quid pro quo* for American promises about the return of
the Ryukyus.

Apart from the bewildering events of the Cultural Revolution, which
looked far more threatening and unpredictable at the time than ten
years later, the first Chinese nuclear explosion in October 1964 had
added a new dimension of uncertainty to Japanese perceptions of
China. Although everyone knew that one successful nuclear test does

not make a nuclear deterrent, a nuclear-armed China had henceforth to be inserted into scenarios of security problems in the future. The combined effect of the Cultural Revolution and of this first nuclear test had a disturbing impact on public opinion in Japan,[6] which suggests that the national mood could swing from one position to another very rapidly under certain provocations.

The need, on the one hand, to adjust to American policy for the sake of national security against external threats and, increasingly, in order to safeguard the very important economic relationship with the United States, and the need, on the other hand, to keep some distance from the United States in east Asia because of different interests and perceptions as well as domestic politics, led to a distinctively Japanese approach in the international politics of the region.

In Asian affairs, Japan became associated with non-communist and anti-communist groupings but tried to avoid being tainted by their strong ideological and anti-Chinese colouring. Nowhere is this better illustrated than in the Asian and Pacific Council (ASPAC), which came into being in 1966 on the initiative of the Republic of Korea. The intention was to concentrate on defending the region against communism. Subsequently, when six of its ten members participated with the US in a conference of the allied belligerents in Vietnam, held in Manila, Foreign Minister Miki countered this development at the second meeting of ASPAC, in July 1967, with a plea for peaceful coexistence with the People's Republic of China. The following year Japan and Singapore prevented anti-communist denunciations by ASPAC, and Miki called for a concentration on economic and cultural affairs in the area. When ASPAC met in Japan in 1969 it was subjected to hostile demonstrations and Miki tried to focus attention on the postwar reconstruction of Indochina.[7]

The Seoul 'tea-party' provided another example of Japanese reserve about the anti-communist crusade. In order to avoid too strong a political tone at a meeting in Seoul, in July 1967, between US Vice-President Humphrey, Vice-President C. K. Yen of the Republic of China, President Park Chung Hee of the Republic of Korea, and Prime Minister Satō, the Japanese side proposed to include wives, thereby turning it into a social occasion.[8]

CHINA IN DOMESTIC POLITICS

The debates over the Treaty of San Francisco and the Peace Treaty with the Republic of China had brought to light the many divisions among the Japanese over China policy. They reflected not only different views about China but different strands of nationalism. These features of the public debate over the China question continued over the next twenty years. The identity of the different groups involved became clearer but the divisions within each increased in profusion and confusion.

At least four identifiable though partly overlapping groups influenced the formulation of Japan's policy towards China after 1952. In ascending order of importance, they are the various opposition parties, business interests, the bureaucracy, and the Liberal-Democratic Party. The opposition parties played an important part in creating a climate of opinion that set the limits within which policy had to operate. The other three groups were more directly involved in policy-making, although none spoke with one voice. I have already suggested that the importance of the business community has often been exaggerated. The bureaucracy wielded more authority – to some extent because of the close ties between senior bureaucrats and politicians of the LDP, but chiefly because the cabinet, which had the ultimate responsibility for decision-making, depended on the bureaucracy to formulate policy owing to the bitter divisions within the government party. The bureaucrats, too, however, were divided amongst themselves over an issue like China.

Before examining each of these groups in turn, it may be useful to take note of the role of public opinion. The structure and mores of Japanese society place a high degree of importance on consensus in the reaching of decisions. It is not the purpose of this study to analyse or explain this phenomenon. That has been done elsewhere on many occasions.[9] The habit of deferring to the movement of opinion or feeling in the group, however it may be gauged, is reflected in official statements which refer to the need to be guided by public opinion or the trend of world opinion on certain matters of policy. Usually it means that there is an irreconcilable clash of opinions within the government and the only way out is to wait for a more propitious moment for its resolution.

While this is undoubtedly true, public opinion has an important if negative function in setting limits and restraints on policy. Normally, popular views on any problem are tested through opinion polls. The Japanese are great addicts of the poll. All the major newspapers conduct them frequently, and the government has its own surveys. The polls vary in quality but provide a rough guide to the state of the public mind on an issue.[10]

Among the many polls on the subject of China, a frequently recurring question related to most-liked and most-disliked foreign countries. The respondent was usually asked to list his three favourite countries in order and the one least liked. China never scored very high in the category of popular countries. In a series of polls taken between 1960 and 1964, no more than 3 to 4 per cent of the respondents looked upon China as one of their favourite countries. Those who disliked China most numbered between 30 and 40 per cent, though they were invariably outnumbered by those who disliked the Soviet Union most. In another poll in 1971, China ranked fifth after the United States, Britain, Switzerland, and the Federal Republic of Germany, as the country to be considered most trustworthy. It was, incidentally, the only Asian country among the first ten preferences.[11]

Such statistics do not speak of any very deep-seated affection or respect for China. They also cast doubt on the extent of Chinese influence on Japanese opinion. The right wing frequently complained of Chinese interference and there is evidence that the Chinese exploited what opportunities were open to them. 'Friendly Trade', the conditions attached to the presence of journalists in Peking, invitations to political, trade union, and cultural personalities, were all designed to play on the competition among commercial enterprises, newspapers, political parties, and groups within a party, to promote a climate of opinion favourable to China and its policies. However, too much can be made of the so-called Chinese influence. National sentiment, which had included a tradition of contempt for China since the nineteenth century, more recently reinforced by pride in Japan's 'economic miracle', was not likely to leave the Japanese very impressed by these efforts. Furthermore, the Japanese resented the superior airs which the Chinese appeared to give themselves. Chinese pronouncements and the conditions the Chinese made for an improvement of relations with Japan revealed a greater concern for establishing the moral superiority of their position than for any subtle manipulation of Japanese sensibilities.

Public opinion, led largely by the press – much less by television – was liable to very sudden swings of mood. It needed only a determined lead from some organ of the press for a 'crowd-effect' to occur and soon all the organs of the media were on the bandwagon. The reason for the quick conformity of the press was the fear of being left behind by one's competitors. The effect was to create a remarkably swift change of mood. Two examples from this period were the uproar over the revision of the Security Treaty and the less dramatic but significant perception of threat after China had exploded its first nuclear device. A third example occurred over normalization of relations with Peking. These sudden eruptions of popular feelings had an important effect on the government but they were rare occurrences. For most of the time, decisions were taken, or not taken, in response to multifarious pressures.

Attitudes towards China in the ruling circles represented no rival schools of thought wedded to particular concepts of the world. They did, however, embody some of the earlier discussion in modern Japan between the 'Mainland' and 'Pacific' schools,[12] as well as the different concepts of nationalism already referred to. They also reflected calculations of political advantage in the constant jockeying for power. They indicated concern for the holder's public image and a desire to be within the compass of the public mood. In some cases they represented links with particular economic interests. It is widely believed that among those most loyal to Taiwan there were some who received subsidies from the Nationalists.

Within the LDP three characteristics were revealed by the absence of any clear alignment on China policy according to factional divisions.[13] Since most of its factions included members who advocated different China policies, efforts to force a change of policy on the government always took the form of 'supra-partisan' membership organizations in the Diet, which included members of several factions of the LDP and the opposition parties. Until 1972 this had been the case of those who sought to steer policy in the direction of Peking. The same phenomenon made its appearance in defence of the interests of the Republic of China after 1972, with the attempt to set up a Japan-Republic of China Relations Dietmen's Consultation Council.

Secondly, individual politicians used relations with China to further their position within the party and in the public eye. This accounts for the promises made by aspirants to the party leadership, only to be quickly forgotten or broken when they assumed office. A new prime minister might have gone on record as determined to make a new approach to Peking. Once faced with the need to satisfy the claims for portfolios from the leaders of those factions who supported him and who usually included ardent partisans of Taipei, he had little hope of implementing dramatic new departures in policy, unless he had ridden in on one of those infrequent waves of the public mood.

From this follows a third characteristic. The internal structure of the ruling party did not allow for policy-making involving controversial issues. It has been observed of the factions, which were 'Built neither on the basis of ideology nor policy,' that 'they are seldom capable of functioning as units of positive and united action.'[14] Paralysed by its structure from establishing a clear line of action, the Liberal-Democratic Party, or rather, the government, was largely dependent on the Foreign Ministry in formulating its position over China. Many more of the pro-Taiwan members of the Party were ex-bureaucrats than those whose sympathies lay in the other direction. Thus, their views tended to be closer to those of the officials in the Foreign Ministry.

A very good example of the Foreign Ministry's role in the formulation of policy is provided by the events that followed de Gaulle's recognition of the PRC. This unleashed a vigorous debate as to whether Japan should follow the French example. The deadlock of opposing views led to an attempt by the Gaimushō to harmonize conflicting views within the Party and bureaucracy through the publication of a 'unified view' on China, on 5 March 1964. (See Appendix C, below.)

The document tried to deal with the consequences of the basic contradiction in Japan's China policy. On the one hand, Japan had a peace treaty with the Nationalist Republic of China, whose government was recognized as the representative of the state of China. On the other hand, Japan had *de facto* relations with the People's Republic of China, in pursuit of its economic interests and for historical and geographical reasons. These relations were justified on the principle of the separation of politics from economics.

The 'unified view' accepted this state of affairs as the one calculated to serve Japan's interests best, but it admitted that the existence of two régimes disputing the sovereignty of China was not 'a normal condition'. A solution could be found only through discussions within the UN and an eventual decision 'in conformity with world opinion'.

This was the guiding principle of those who drafted the document. They described the problem of Chinese representation within the UN as an 'important question' and not merely a 'simple and formal' matter. They indicated that Japan would accept the verdict of the UN and would in all likelihood establish diplomatic relations with Peking once it had been seated in the world organization. The process of admitting the People's Republic of China to the UN was pointedly linked to a condition, i.e. 'when it is proved that it is necessary and desirable for the maintenance of peace in Asia and in the world.'

The middle section of the three-point 'unified view' was devoted to a discussion of whether Communist China posed a threat to peace. While the authors saw no immediate military threat and stated that 'China takes a prudent attitude towards the outside world', they saw a distinct ideological threat and, in particular, an attempt to destroy the Japan-US security system. After taking a side-swipe at the idea of a neutralist and disarmed Japan, the section finishes with a warning against Chinese attempts to turn the Japanese public against Taiwan and the United States by raising a 'pro-China mood'.

In conclusion, the authors of the document thought it much too early for Japan to decide on its position in the forthcoming China debate at the UN that autumn, arguing that it would be premature to assume that the French recognition of Peking would have a decisive effect on Chinese representation at the UN. None the less, the gist of the document made it clear that only a substantial majority for the PRC, including the United States, would cause Japan to alter its policy.

Three points are worth noting in connection with the 'unified view'. Henceforth, as the seating of Peking in the UN gained ever more adherents, the Japanese were to insist that they would be guided by the climate of world opinion. Secondly, the guidelines laid down in 1964 were substantially adhered to seven years later. Lastly, it reflected a continued emphasis on the existence of two Chinese governments, although the text is somewhat ambiguous, referring occasionally to Taiwan. Indeed, the document carefully avoided any mention of a two Chinas or one China/one Taiwan solution. However, the officials in the Foreign Ministry who were in charge of Chinese affairs hoped that Peking and Taipei would eventually accept the implications of a two Chinas policy.

The 'unified view' is an example of bureaucrats stepping in to formulate policy when the politicians alone would have failed. It bears the imprint of Gaimushō bias towards the American alliance and concern with security. The heavy emphasis on accepting the trend of world opinion was one way of indicating alignment with American policy, as the United States could still command a majority in the UN at that time. It is also an interesting example of the transfer of a cultural characteristic to the international scene. Consensus, meaning a clear trend of opinion or indication of mood, is indispensable before a decision can be reached in Japan. Hence, the function of the UN as a sounding-board of world opinion is important for the Japanese in adjusting their foreign policy.

The influence of the Gaimushō might not have been so great if the business world had been more united over the question of relations with Peking. The role of business interests has been discussed earlier in this chapter. Here it need only be added that, narrowly focused as they were on their economic and commercial interests and their competitive standing, the leaders of business did not exert consistent or sustained pressure on the authorities. And since the Japanese economy was so closely tied to that of the United States in the 1950s and 1960s, it was all the easier for the Foreign Ministry to persuade the government to follow a line of extreme caution in its dealings with China.

The slightest sign of displeasure from the United States was enough to halt any groping towards improved relations with Peking. Even when the United States was not opposed to a project, as in January 1964 when the Chinese proposed a direct air service between China and Japan, the officials of the Gaimushō effectively opposed it; this in spite of the fact that their Minister, Shiina, had said it was a 'good idea' and the Minister at the American Embassy let it be known that there would be no objection from the American side. A proposal to bring a Chinese trade delegation to Tokyo by a Japanese chartered plane in March 1964 was again vetoed by government officials.

The Gaimushō may have played a key role on occasion, as in the formulation of the 'unified view' of March 1964, but that is not to say that it had its own way. China policy involved conflicting views between ministries and within ministries. Some officials of the Foreign Ministry, for instance, favoured a more positive approach towards Peking. So it is not strictly accurate to speak of *the* Foreign Ministry view on China, although the dominant faction favoured Taiwan. The Gaimushō's perspective on international relations extended beyond the commercial balance sheet. Preoccupied with political and security problems, its principal concern was to maintain the special relationship with the United States. Hence, it protested in September 1963 when two officials accompanied a Japanese trade mission to Peking.

The pressure from MITI was, on the whole, in the opposite direction. In January 1965 a MITI official was appointed head of the permanent Japanese trade mission in Peking, after he had resigned his position as chief of the General Affairs Bureau. Since economic factors were a key element in Japan's relations with China, it is not surprising that MITI sometimes had the edge over the Gaimushō in imposing its views on the government.

In all this it is important to remember that differences over China policy often reflected more mundane bureaucratic rivalries. Competition over which ministry or which bureau within a ministry was to have charge of implementing a particular policy or decision played as large a role as differences in outlook, and possibly even a larger role.

Finally, a word about the role of the opposition parties, all of which leaned towards Peking to a greater or less degree. Their influence was, however, weakened by divisions within each party, and, again, between the parties.

Within the Japan Socialist Party (JSP) – the largest of the opposition parties – there was no more unity concerning the People's Republic of China than within the LDP. Opinions varied according to faction, but not wholly so. The larger or leadership factions, in particular, displayed a considerable variation in outlook. Early clashes within the party over whether Japan should ally itself with the West or pursue a policy of neutralism and alignment with Asian nationalism, were in the tradition of the national debate between the 'Pacific' and 'Mainland' schools. The founding of the Democratic-Socialist Party (DSP) in 1960 had been motivated in part by a reaction against the pro-communism of the party's dominant factions. Subsequent intra-party struggles also centred on basic foreign policy issues, including China policy. These were more ideological than diplomatic, as the party consistently rejected a two Chinas or one China/one Taiwan policy.

The Japan Communist Party was as much prone to factionalism and in-fighting as the other Japanese parties, but its position was further complicated by its ties with the world communist movement. In the 1950s the Party was under Peking's influence, partly because many of the leaders had close personal associations with the Chinese and partly because the Russians were not very active in Asia. Chinese policy, with its focus on American 'imperialism' and national liberation, appealed more to the Japanese than the Russian emphasis on class struggle and the defeat of capitalism. The emotional and sentimental pull of China on Japanese minds undoubtedly also played its part.

In the first phase of the great communist schism, until 1961, the Party, like the parties in Vietnam and Indonesia, tried to remain neutral, which pleased neither the Russians nor the Chinese. Between 1961 and 1964 the JCP drifted towards the Chinese side and in March 1964 it broke openly with the Russians at a meeting of the two parties in Moscow. By 1966 the Japanese communists were also at loggerheads with the Chinese comrades. They had been shocked by the Chinese incitement of the Indonesian Party in its abortive coup of September 1965, by their opposition to international united action over Vietnam, and by Mao's insistence that the JCP should resort to arms in its struggle for power rather than rely on the parliamentary process. This last rankled most, for the Japanese communists were no exception to their countrymen in their resentment at being read high-minded lectures on political morality, or any subject, by the Chinese.

The positions of the JSP and JCP were diametrically opposed in the 1960s. In 1964 the communists were close to Peking while the JSP leant towards Moscow in the Sino-Soviet dispute. In 1967 the JCP was at daggers drawn with the Chinese party, while the JSP espoused its cause. In doing so, the socialist leaders may have calculated that the promotion of a pro-Chinese policy would not only attract those supporters of the JCP whose sympathies lay in that direction but would also attract wider public support, including that of business interests favourably disposed to the People's Republic, although without specific ideological preferences. The JSP pursued the same tactics as the other parties and the anti-mainstream factions of the LDP in exploiting the attraction that the China issue, as distinct from China itself, exercised over so many Japanese.

From the perspective of domestic politics, it is clear that in spite of the wide appeal of a more friendly approach to the People's Republic of China, official policy favoured the Kuomintang. Nevertheless, even the most ardent friends of the Kuomintang always sought to keep up some relationship with the People's Republic of China. One reason for avoiding an out-and-out commitment to Taiwan was the delicate balance of power within the LDP.

c

It is generally true that the pro-Taiwan element was numerically stronger and politically more significant in that it provided many of the leading ministers throughout this period. Moreover, those ministers who were not openly identified with the cause of the Chinese Nationalists, were inclined to take a non-committal rather than a pro-Peking position. Yet those whose interests inclined them to champion the mainland government were strong enough to moderate the Japanese position sufficiently so that at no time, not even during the most severe crisis, was there a total rupture between the two countries as there had been between the United States and the People's Republic of China.

The real strength of the pro-Peking elements lay in the fact that they could count on the support of the opposition parties, most of the national press, and an articulate section of public opinion. They could thus threaten to embarrass the government over an area of policy in which it wanted to avoid a serious confrontation. They were aided further by the absence of a vigorous stand on the part of the business community, although its leadership was generally sympathetic to Taiwan. Finally, occasional interventions by the Chinese also marginally helped their cause.

CONCLUSION

The issues which emerged in the debate over policy towards China between 1949 and 1952 were, to a large extent, a prefiguration of the issues which dominated China policy in the following twenty years. The categories still held in 1971 but their dimensions had changed. In trade, economic realities had dispelled the dream, but economic relations with Peking had assumed a political importance quite out of proportion to their commercial value, which represented a tiny fraction of Japan's foreign trade.

Although the issue of Taiwan became the biggest stumbling-block in the way of the normalization of relations with Peking, the trend of Japanese policy was towards accommodation with both Chinese governments. The recognition of two Chinas was seen as the best solution. None the less, Japan's commitment to the Chiang Kai-shek régime became increasingly entangled with national security policy.

The problem of national security had changed over the years. The 'Chinese threat' was no longer conceived as part of a monolithic communist threat, and it gradually ceased to be identified with subversion. Instead, these perceptions were replaced by a feeling of uncertainty about China, heightened by the Cultural Revolution and the nuclear tests. Unease about China's unpredictability was one reason, fear of the Soviet Union was obviously another, which strengthened the case for the American alliance.* On the other hand, the war in Indochina created unease about the direction of American policy and the dangers of Japan's involvement in it.

A desire not to be wholly identified with the United States and the continued need of American protection between them account for an independent but very cautious Japanese line over a number of issues in international politics. The most significant example of this cautious independence was Japan's interest in relations with the Mainland, openly or tacitly fostered by the government throughout twenty years of Sino-American confrontation.

The government's openness towards such contacts was, of course, due in large measure to domestic pressures. The line-up of groups in support of either Peking or Taipei followed the pattern that had emerged under the Occupation and did not conform strictly to the divisions between Left and Right in Japanese politics. The crosscurrents that the China issue introduced into domestic politics were strengthened by the effect of the Sino-Soviet schism on the communist and socialist parties. Nevertheless, China was exploited as a political issue by the opposition parties and the pro-Peking elements in the LDP. They used it to mobilize nationalist sentiment against the government and their chief target was the association with the United States. Those who supported that association were no less nationalist but their nationalism did not have the emotional appeal of a racialism which stressed the common 'Asianism' of the Japanese and Chinese.

The public debate over policy towards China gave the impression that the government slavishly followed American policy. The processes by which decisions were reached and formulated gave the impression that Japanese policy was passive and reactive. Neither impression was correct.

It is of course true that Japan did everything to avoid any serious conflict with the United States, and it is true that Japanese policy was reactive – that applies to the foreign policy of any country. But it is not true that there was no distinctive Japanese approach to the China question nor that it was not given expression in action.

The primary purpose in foreign policy between 1952 and 1971 was to keep open as many options as possible in relations with the rest of the world. There were at least three main reasons for such an approach. First, the balance of domestic political forces favoured a vague, and,

* Whereas American and Western writers generally refer to the Japan-US relationship as an 'alliance', the Japanese do not use that word when referring to it. This seems to indicate a somewhat different concept of their association with the United States. While bearing this in mind, I have occasionally used the term 'alliance' for the sake of convenience.

as far as possible, non-committal foreign policy. Secondly, there was no wish to be left naked should the protective cover of the United States ever be removed. Thirdly, and this became essential after the great economic upsurge in the 1960s, Japan's interests dictated friendly relations with the whole world. The handling of the China issue bears the marks of this approach to external relations. When the change came, it was no accident that, after initial confusion, Japan overtook the United States in the scope of its new relationship with China.

NOTES

1 There exists an abundant literature on Japan's postwar economy. G. C. Allen, *A Short Economic History of Modern Japan* (London, Allen & Unwin, 2nd rev. edn., 1962) is an excellent survey of economic development since the Meiji Restoration and concludes with a useful chapter on the first fifteen years of the postwar era. *Consider Japan*, by a group of journalists of *The Economist* (London, Duckworth, 1963), is a perceptive analysis of how the foundations were laid for the country's remarkable economic growth in the 1960s. G. C. Allen, *Japan's Place in Trade Strategy; Larger Role in Pacific Region* (London, The Atlantic Trade Study, July 1968) deals with the changing structures and patterns of external trade. Angus Maddison, *Economic Growth in Japan and the USSR* (London, Allen & Unwin, 1969) contains a revealing discussion of the causes of Japan's economic success.

2 Katō Y., *Zaikai* (Tokyo, Kawade Shobō, 1966), ch. 7.

3 The discussion of the significance of the *gyōkai* is based on conversations with Mrs Ogata Sadako and Professor Hosoya Chihiro. Mrs Ogata has contributed a chapter on 'The Business Community and Japanese Foreign Policy: Normalization of Relations with the People's Republic of China' to Robert A. Scalapino, ed., *The Foreign Policy of Japan* (Berkeley, Univ. of California Press, 1977), pp. 175–203. Unfortunately, I have not had a chance to read the book before finishing this work.

4 See Etō S., 'An Outline of Formosan History', in M. Mancall, ed., *Formosa Today* (New York, Praeger, 1964), pp. 43–58.

5 See ibid., J. Ong, 'A Formosan's View of the Formosan Independence Movement', pp. 166, 169–70. Also, Lung-chu Chen and Harold Lasswell, *Formosa, China, and the United Nations: Formosa in the World Community* (New York, St. Martin's Press, 1967), pp. 194–6; Sheldon L. Appleton, 'Taiwan: Portents of Change', *Asian Survey*, vol. XI, no. 1, Jan 1971, pp. 69–70.

6 The Chinese nuclear test of 1964 led the LDP to consider its implication for national security. Public opinion polls conducted by the *Yomiuri Shimbun* and *Mainichi Shimbun* in 1967, 1968, and 1969 also revealed a considerable increase in the percentage of respondents who had become anxious about 'the Chinese threat'. The percentage dropped quite sharply when the Cultural Revolution seemed to be dying down and

there were signs of a movement towards *rapprochement* with China. John E. Endicott, *Japan's Nuclear Option: Political, Technical, and Strategic Factors* (New York, Praeger, 1975), pp. 55–8, 97, 101, 111–12, n. 251.

7 Frank Langdon, *Japan's Foreign Policy* (Vancouver, Univ. of British Columbia Press, 1973), pp. 188–9. Japan reluctantly joined ASPAC in 1966, and only after the Thais and South Koreans had agreed to tone down its anti-communism. A Japanese diplomat is reported to have said, 'We are on the extreme left in ASPAC.' Robert E. Osgood and others, *Japan and the United States in Asia* (Baltimore, Md, Johns Hopkins Press, 1968), pp. 36–8. Foreign Minister Aichi again underlined Japan's position at the special Asian and Pacific Conference on the situation in Cambodia, which was convened in Djakarta on 16 May 1970. He said that the purpose of the conference was to seek peace and not to form a group based on a particular political stand. He deliberately dissociated Japan from criticism of the North Vietnamese and Vietcong invasion of Cambodia. *Japan Quarterly*, vol. XVII, no. 3, July–Sep 1970, p. 350.

8 Osgood and others, pp. 36–8.

9 The processes whereby decisions are reached in Japan have attracted a good deal of attention from political and social scientists since the war. One of the most recent books on the subject is a series of case studies edited by Ezra F. Vogel, *Modern Japanese Organization and Decision Making* (Berkeley, Univ. of California Press, 1975).

10 Among the opinion surveys conducted by the press, those of the *Asahi* are probably the most reliable. Polls are a separate department of a newspaper, and working on them means that the journalist is outside the promotion route. They are, therefore, unpopular assignments and shunned by the ambitious and able. Moreover, every paper is financially in the red and as polls are an expensive item they are subject to distorting economies. Editorial policy also affects the wording of questions and accounts for the omission of material which does not suit the paper's outlook. A substantial amount of the data collected is never published. Although government-sponsored polls are fairly reliable, they, too, operate on a tight budget. Several surveys may be combined, with the result that the interviewees are peppered with too many questions and easily become tired and confused. See also, Tanaka Yasumasa, 'The Change and Continuity in Contemporary Japanese Society as Shown in Opinion Polls between 1946 and 1972', *Gakushuin Review of Law and Politics*, no. 8, 1972.

11 Irie Michimasa, 'Communist China's Nuclear Power and the Security of Japan', *Journal of Social and Political Ideas in Japan*, vol. III, no. 2, Aug 1965, pp. 19–21; *Yomiuri*, 19 Oct 1971.

12 This refers to the debate which had been going on almost since the Meiji Restoration but was particularly acute at the turn of the century, about the fundamental orientation of Japan's foreign policy. The 'Mainland' school favoured a forward policy in Asia, with Japan leading Asian resistance against the imperialist powers of the West – a euphemism for

the establishment of Japanese domination. The 'Pacific' school, on the other hand, argued that Japan's destiny was that of a maritime power and policy should, therefore, be orientated towards the other naval powers in the Pacific – Britain and the United States.

13 Fukui, *Party in Power*, p. 256, Table 27.
14 Ibid., p. 266.

3 The Diplomatic Revolution of 1971—1972 and Subsequent Policy

THE announcement on 15 July 1971 that President Nixon would visit China in the spring of 1972 surprised Tokyo. As early as January, the Japanese had been aware that something was afoot[1] and they faced a dilemma : on the one hand, they had to avoid taking sides with China and running the risk of a break with the United States; on the other, they had to avoid becoming the victims of an American-Chinese understanding. None the less, they were shocked by the three minutes' notice given to them before Nixon's historic announcement.

The immediate reaction of pained surprise hinted at betrayal by a trusted partner. The implication was that Japan's loyalty to its 'elder brother', or 'senior partner', had been shamefully repaid. There is evidence to suggest that this explanation of the 'shock' was more of a public relations exercise than the real reason for Japanese annoyance. They had been caught on the hop and there was anxiety over Japan's isolation at a time of rapid change in the international environment.

While the opposition within and outside the LDP launched into a chorus of 'we told you so', the government and those close to it made a virtue of necessity and insisted that henceforth Japan must pursue its own policy, should not react hastily, and should be guided by strictly calculated national interest. Just to prove that Japan could act independently – and to give vent to injured self-respect – the government took a unilateral decision over dollar convertibility in the Ryukyus without notifying the United States in advance. It made Satō feel good because he had 'jumped over the head' of the United States.[2] The drive for an autonomous policy had started at the beginning of the 1950s, but the American action in 1971 had presented an opportunity for which the Japanese were at first unprepared.

THE MOVEMENT TOWARDS NORMALIZATION
JULY 1971 TO SEPTEMBER 1972

For a general view of the main developments during this year, the reader is invited to refer to the chronology at Appendix E below. He will notice that Japanese progress on the road to Peking was a two-speed affair. Businessmen were much quicker to move than the politicians. The reasons are not far to seek.

By the end of the 1960s Japanese business was running into difficulties with its American trade. From 1965 onwards the United States had rapidly mounted an enormous deficit in its trade with Japan. It was not long before protectionist pressures made themselves felt on the American political scene. In 1969 began the bitter and protracted wrangle between the two countries over Japanese textile exports, the object of much misunderstanding and a direct cause of the deteriorating political climate between them.

Many Japanese manufacturers and traders were, therefore, especially alert for opportunities to export elsewhere and watched the Chinese market closely. What really alarmed them was the prospect that their rivals at home might steal a march to Peking and that other industrialized countries might capture the market before them. In 1970, for instance, it was feared that Italy, which had recognized the People's Republic of China on 5 November, might gain an advantage in the export of chemical fertilizers. These fears were confirmed in 1971, when the Japanese fertilizer manufacturers concluded an agreement with the Chinese after very arduous negotiations and on terms less favourable than in previous years.

What added to the attraction of the Chinese market was the existence of two factors which were considered as favourable to the Japanese interest. China's trade with Russia and East Europe was declining and the closure of the Suez Canal in 1967 had added to the cost and delay of deliveries from West Europe.

The Chinese were surely not unaware of the heightened interest of Japanese business circles, and, true to their policy of seeking political leverage through economic relations, seized the opportunity of further weakening the Japanese position over Taiwan and other issues. Accordingly, the Memorandum Trade Agreement signed on 1 March 1971, reiterated the three principles and the inseparability of economics and politics as the basis of relations between the two sides. It also defined the four categories of 'factories, firms, and enterprises' with which the Chinese would not trade : (1) those 'helping the Chiang Kai-shek gang stage a comeback to the Mainland' and those helping the South Korean régime 'intrude into the Democratic People's Republic of Korea'; (2)

those with large investments in Taiwan and South Korea; (3) those supplying arms and ammunition to the Americans for use in Indochina; (4) all American-Japanese joint enterprises or Japanese subsidiaries of American companies.[3]

Almost immediately after the Nixon announcement, the Japanese made a rapid succession of moves. In August the Kansai Committee for Economic Development (Dōyūkai) called for a radical revision of Japanese policy in favour of the People's Republic of China. In the bureaucracy, MITI was the first to react by lifting bans on the import of primary products from China, North Korea, North Vietnam, East Germany, Albania, and Mongolia. It also set up a new Japan-People's Republic of China Trade Office in its International Bureau. Day after day, the press reported new deals with the Chinese, decisions to stop attending meetings with the Nationalist Chinese and South Koreans, planned missions of business leaders to Peking, concessions by the Japanese authorities over trade with the Mainland. Thus, after extending a yen credit to Taiwan on 9 August 1971, the government suspended it four days later because it feared the repercussions on trade with China.

One indicator of the rush was provided by the demand for places at the autumnal Canton Trade Fair, held from 15 October to 15 November 1971. In the spring fair of that year 791 companies and 1408 persons had participated. By the beginning of October the number of firms taking part had risen to 1457 with a total of 2300 representatives.[4] However, not every firm saw the need for hurry. Matsushita's Vice-President Takahashi Aratarō, for instance, saw no point in severing its ties with Taiwan because China offered no market for the sophisticated electrical appliances produced by Japanese industry.[5]

The Chinese for their part hastened the process of accommodation by a characteristically pragmatic application of the policy which was supposed to have been based on a number of principles. Thus, the Toyota Motor Company was able to enter into commercial relations with China in spite of an 80 per cent share in the South Korean automobile market and a link with the Korean and Taiwanese automobile industries. Hitachi had no difficulty in accepting the principles of trade laid down by the Chinese, in spite of substantial investments in Taiwan. However, Teijin, a leading textile manufacturer whose stake in Taiwan was about the same as that of Hitachi, was snubbed by Peking. On the other hand, Shin Nippon Steel was acceptable to the Chinese in spite of its involvement in a huge steel project at Pohang in the Republic of Korea. The Chinese justified this apparent anomaly on the grounds that Shin Nippon Steel was regarded as helping the people of Korea rather than supporting the Republic of Korea's 'military aggression'.[6] On the whole, Peking was willing to overlook existing stakes in Taiwan and Korea, provided there were no plans for further investments.

Whereas, through their economic policy, the Chinese assiduously promoted a political climate which would lead to the isolation and weakening of Taiwan, to the undermining of Mr Satō's authority, and to a basic shift in Japanese policy, Japanese business interests were almost wholly concerned with economic motives. For some, like Toyota, it was a matter of getting into the Chinese market ahead of the big three American car giants.[7] For others, like Tokyo Shibaura Electric Company (Tōshiba), it was a question of beating Japanese rivals. Still other companies attempted to offset major losses in sales and profits. By the end of the year the president of Keidanren, the most powerful and influential of the four major Japanese economic organizations, called for the normalization of relations with the People's Republic of China as soon as possible.

One result of the rush to Peking was a tendency among the big firms to continue economic relations with Taiwan less obtrusively. For example, Chou En-lai received a delegation from the Mitsubishi group of companies in August 1972 while the chairman of Mitsubishi Heavy Industries was vising Taiwan in the same month. The Japanese government tended to do things the other way round. Official relations with Taipei were upheld but there were many overtures to Peking.

Conflicts within the LDP and tension between it and the Foreign Ministry accounted for confused and hesitant reactions to the American initiative. On 20 July Mr Satō stressed that the authorities in Taipei were the sole 'legitimate' government of China and that there could be no question of abolishing the Treaty of Peace signed with the Republic of China. The next day he declared his readiness to go to Peking and to recognize the People's Republic on condition that this did not mean the ouster of Taiwan from the UN.

In these early days of the diplomatic revolution in east Asia, official spokesmen emphasized the need for consensus within the ruling party and between it and the Foreign Ministry, without which the government could not clarify its policy. Nevertheless, Mr Satō gradually inched his way towards a fundamental break with previous policy. On 10 September 1971 he spoke of the need for a 'one China' formula which recognized the reality of governments in Peking and Taipei, which was intended both to meet Peking's strenuous objections to the 'two Chinas' policy and to make sure that both Chinese governments were represented in the UN. The government reversed Foreign Minister Aichi's position of December 1970 and did, after all, co-sponsor a resolution with the US at the UN, making the China issue an 'important question'. However, it supported the seating of both Chinese governments and the transfer of the seat in the Security Council to Peking.[8] At last, on 6 March 1972, Foreign Minister Fukuda Takeo was able to present the government's 'unified view' on mainland China and Taiwan. Referring to the Treaty of San Francisco, he stated that Japan had no right to pronounce on the territorial status of Taiwan. However, the government declared that the position of the People's Republic was fully understandable and that it would seek to normalize relations on this basis. Two months later Fukuda removed another obstacle by announcing that the reference to Taiwan in the Satō-Nixon communiqué of 1969 had ceased to be relevant after the publication of the Chou-Nixon communiqué of 27 February 1972.

This was as far as the government could go. The Chinese had made it abundantly clear that there was no prospect of establishing diplomatic relations as long as Mr Satō was at the helm. Accordingly, when Mr Tanaka became prime minister on 7 July 1972, Peking let it be known a week later that he had passed the test of acceptability by showing 'perfect understanding' of the three principles laid down as the conditions for the establishment of diplomatic relations. They were : (1) recognition of Peking as the sole legal government of China; (2) recognition of Taiwan as part of China; (3) abrogation of the Treaty between Japan and the Republic of China and severance of diplomatic relations with Taiwan.

Before going to Peking at the end of September, Mr Tanaka met President Nixon in Honolulu. Significantly, there was no mention of Taiwan in the subsequent communiqué. Their conversation had confirmed a parting of the ways. Japan was prepared to sever official relations with Taiwan, the United States would not do so.

The general picture of disarray in government policy that emerged between July 1971 and July 1972 was expressed in the mutual recriminations of the leaders of the LDP and officials of the Gaimushō. The politicians accused the officials of failing to warn them of impending American moves, of completely misjudging the international situation, and of acting with total disregard for the domestic situation in Japan. The officials' excuse was that Mr Satō had been indecisive and contradictory over the China question and that since it was a high-level political problem, it should have been handled by the highest ranking political leaders.

The politicians of the LDP may have been right that the Foreign Ministry, always conscious of the importance of the special relationship with the United States, was remiss in not giving enough attention to the alternatives for Japan in the event of a major change in American policy without prior consultation or warning. But when they accused the officials of failing to take account of the political situation at home, they pointed to the real weakness in policy-making, which lay in the LDP.

The inability of its leaders to formulate a clear position over the China problem was due to the composition and structure of the Party as described in the previous chapter. The usual difficulties of reaching agreement were accentuated by the manœuvring and bargaining which preceded the election of a new party president, and therefore prime minister, in July 1972. The details of the in-fighting need not concern us here, but adjustment of individual positions over the China issue was often made for corresponding concessions over matters which had nothing to do with China.[9]

Within the Party as a whole it was impossible to make a clear-cut division between those who were pro-Peking, those who were pro-Taipei, and those who took a non-aligned position. In each group there was a delicate shading of views which often merged into those of one of the other categories. The confusion and the plethora of viewpoints are well illustrated in an analysis of individual reactions to a draft resolution submitted by the chairman of the LDP's China Problem Research Council at its meeting in October 1971.[10] The draft resolution consisted of four parts, which may be summarized as follows:

(1) The government of the People's Republic of China represents China.
(2) Taiwan is part of China's territory and therefore China is one.
(3) The existence of two Chinese governments is a 'historical reality'. The people of China must decide what to do about this problem.
(4) The Japanese government should take appropriate measures to normalize relations with China.

According to press reports, the members of the Council reacted in a variety of ways. One questioned the first two points and doubted if Taiwan was a part of China. Another wanted the third point revised so that the resolution would not contradict the China vote at the United Nations. Fujiyama Aiichirō[11] agreed with the first two points but wanted number three omitted completely. Ikeda Masanosuke[12] merely wanted the word 'historical' omitted from that part of the resolution. Yet another member suggested that the 'restoration of diplomatic relations' be substituted for 'normalization' in part four. Some agreed with this but did not want any assertive position to be taken on the territorial issue. Kaya Okinori[13] thought all paragraphs debatable and agreed only with the preamble.

Two members advocated delay in the absence of consensus. One felt that it was basically a problem of international law and that a policy should be decided through holding talks with the United States.

Another, Nakao Eiichi,[14] suggested caution and no definite commitment so as to ensure as much support as possible for the resolution in the Diet.

All the vacillations and prevarications quickly disappeared once Mr Tanaka had taken over the leadership of the Party and the country on 7 July 1972. Within less than three months he was in Peking to establish diplomatic relations with the People's Republic of China. The speed of adjustment was undoubtedly influenced by the ground-swell of public opinion which created a national mood in favour of such a step. Immediately after the announcement of Mr Nixon's impending visit to China, acting Foreign Minister Kimura Toshio had said that the government could not move without a clear indication of such a mood. He went even further and suggested that 'Public opinion should lead government policy.'[15]

The 'mood' had been growing for some time before the events discussed in this chapter. A public opinion survey conducted in March 1968 had revealed 52·7 per cent of the respondents as favouring an early restoration of diplomatic relations. When this figure was broken down according to party allegiance, supporters of the LDP were the least numerous (48·4 per cent), but not far behind those of the Kōmei Party (52·1 per cent).[16] The events from July 1971 onwards, however, really caused a landslide. An *Asahi* poll in May 1971 had asked the interviewees to name the countries with which they wanted Japan to be on friendly terms; the United States scored 39 per cent and China 21 per cent. The same question asked seven months later reversed the order, with 33 per cent mentioning China and 28 per cent the United States.[17] An interesting sample of the state of public opinion on the eve of normalization was obtained in a poll published by *Sankei Shimbun* on 28 July 1972. Eighty-two per cent were favourable to moving ahead with normalization, but 72·2 per cent wanted to retain trade relations and the exchange of persons (i.e. tourism) with Taiwan, although only 2·6 per cent wanted to maintain existing relations (i.e. recognition as the government of China) with it.[18]

The exact relationship between the formulation of official policy and the effect of public opinion is as difficult to determine as the chicken-and-egg conundrum. However, there can be no doubt that the shift of the national mood had an important influence and this may be observed in the subtle shifts of the opposition parties in spite of their general predisposition towards Peking.

Reading from right to left among the parties, the Democratic-Socialist Party changed its policy after a leadership struggle. Hitherto, its approach to China had scarcely differed from those in the centre of the LDP. It had maintained that recognition of the People's Republic should not mean repudiation of Taiwan, whose ultimate fate should be decided through a referendum among the people. In November 1971 the new party line was clearly established in accordance with the principles laid down by Peking. Proof that the DSP had worked its passage came with an invitation to send a delegation to Peking in the spring of 1972 – the first it had ever received.[19]

Kōmeitō had consistently followed a line in support of diplomatic relations with Peking but had remained studiously vague about the processes and terms under which they should be established. A joint statement issued by the China-Japan Friendship Association and a Kōmeitō delegation in Peking on 2 July 1971 brought it into line with the Chinese position over Taiwan.[20]

The JSP had the least difficulty in adjusting its policy, but the communists were in a dilemma because of their differences with Peking, which had consigned them to outer darkness alongside Mr Satō. The JCP was conspicuously absent from the various supra-partisan pro-Peking campaigns. The Party's inability to join the rush to Peking did not apparently affect its standing with the electorate in December 1972, when the largest number of communists was returned to the Lower House of the Diet since 1949.

NORMALIZATION

Mr Tanaka went to Peking on 25 September 1972 and four days later, on 29 September, the Chou-Tanaka communiqué announced to the world that Japan had established diplomatic relations with the People's Republic of China. (See Appendix D, below.)

The communiqué stated that Japan fully understood and respected the position that 'Taiwan is an inalienable part of the territory of the People's Republic of China.' This was in contrast to Italy and Canada, which had only 'taken note' of the Chinese position. Japan reaffirmed its adherence to Article (8) of the Potsdam Proclamation, which had referred to the Cairo Declaration with its specific intention of restoring Formosa to China. The Cairo Declaration concerned the Republic of China, but in the communiqué of 1972 the Japanese side stated that it 'proceeds from the stand of fully understanding the three principles for the restoration of diplomatic relations put forward by the Government of the People's Republic of China.'

It has been said that the Japanese position is sufficiently vague in the text of the communiqué as to leave open Japan's options over Taiwan. In support of this, one may point to the use of the words 'understand' and 'respect' rather than 'accept' or 'agree' with reference to the Chinese position. Hence, the Japanese made no categoric commitment either over Taiwan or over the three principles. Secondly, there is only one specific mention of Taiwan in the whole text. Finally, there is no specific mention of the Japan-Republic of China Treaty, nor of the need to abrogate it.

A textual analysis of the communiqué would, therefore, suggest that the Japanese retained some latitude in their future policy towards Taiwan. This is to some extent confirmed by what is known of the difficulties which emerged during the course of the negotiations over its wording. The Japanese side wanted a vague formula as far as their relations with Taiwan were concerned. The Chinese wanted a clear statement of intent. In the end, Peking accepted vagueness in return for some promise from the Japanese that they would clarify their relations with Taiwan in subsequent statements.

This happened only partially. At a press conference immediately after the signing of the Chou-Tanaka communiqué, Foreign Minister Ōhira stressed three points : the 1952 Treaty between Japan and the Republic of China had lost its *raison d'être* and was terminated; Japan would have to close its embassy in Taipei in the 'not too distant' future; since Japan had accepted the Cairo and Potsdam Declarations, it was 'natural' for Japan 'to consider Taiwan as part of China's territory'.[21] That same morning, the Japanese vice-minister for Foreign Affairs had told Taiwan's ambassador in Tokyo that the establishment of relations with the People's Republic of China meant that Japan could no longer maintain diplomatic relations with Taiwan. Yet he expressed the hope that trade ties between the two countries would continue. In the evening, the government in Taipei took the initiative and severed relations.

In doing so, the government of Taiwan relieved the Japanese of the need to perform this painful action. Ever since that date, the Japanese government has scrupulously avoided any formal and precise declaration of its relationship with Taiwan. Its basic attitude was summed up by Mr Ōhira in his reply to a question about future relations with Taiwan, which was put to him by the political editor of *The Japan Times* on 30 September 1972 : 'We hope to continue economic and cultural relations with Taiwan. But that will depend on how Taiwan reacts to Japan's new relations with China. So we have to wait and see.'[22]

The government's unwillingness to make a clear and unequivocal stand was further reflected in Mr Tanaka's statement to a group of business leaders a fortnight later. He told them that the communiqué of 29 September had not indicated final agreement between the People's Republic of China and Japan over Japan's relations with Taiwan. On 31 October he told the Diet that : 'We can no longer maintain diplomatic ties with Taiwan, but the Government will make sure that the exchange of visits, trade and other relations are continued at a private level.'[23] In this context, the question of long-term export credits would be 'carefully studied'.

However, there is another interpretation of the Chou-Tanaka communiqué, which maintains that, far from allowing Japan to retain a freedom of choice in its relations with Taiwan, 'China yielded nothing of substance but merely made some concessions on wording and phrasing.'[24] Moreover, it is interesting to note that in the series of communiqués signed by the Chinese and the various Japanese delegations prior to Mr Tanaka's visit to Peking, it was the Japanese and not the Chinese who had insisted on the importance of immediate acceptance of the three principles. At home, the opposition parties and the pro-Peking members of the LDP had also exercised pressure in this direction.

The Japanese approach to the negotiations is, therefore, seen to resemble the traditional 'oriental' method, as depicted in the relations between the Chinese Empire and its tributaries. Japan accepted China's superior position by agreeing beforehand to the principles which were to govern the conduct of the relationship between them. Thus she hoped to reap advantages in practical terms, very much in line with the tradition whereby the tribute-receiving authority bestowed 'gifts' of greater value on the tributary than it received.[25] If this is so, it suggests that Taiwan has a greater symbolic than strategic significance for the Chinese.

Although there were many in the government, especially in the Foreign Ministry, who opposed this stance, the government's choice of intermediaries in the preliminary exchanges made this posture inevitable in the final negotiations. The emissaries included not only LDP politicians, for example Furui Yoshimi, who were sympathetic to the People's Republic, but leaders of the opposition parties, such as Takeiri Yoshikatsu of Kōmeitō[26] and Sasaki Kōzō, a former Chairman of the Socialist Party. In addition, the Director of the Trade Memorandum Office in Tokyo, Okazaki Kaheita, strongly advocated this line.

As far as the actual gains from the normalization of relations were concerned, honours were more or less even. Both sides achieved some objectives and both sides made sufficient concessions to leave the course of future relations open, to be manipulated by each party in the light of changing circumstances and interests. The Japanese certainly lost face on the moral side, in that they not only appeared to bow to China's superior position but had in fact been forced publicly to betray their friendship with the government in Taiwan.

The ease of accommodation between Peking and Tokyo also had its causes in each party's perception of the immediate international situation. We can guess at some of the reasons why the Chinese might have been anxious to make a settlement as quickly as possible, though they are not the main concern of this study. They probably included worries about Soviet intentions, heightened by Mr Gromyko's visit to Tokyo in January 1972 and the resulting agreement that Soviet-Japanese negotiations to conclude a peace treaty should be initiated that year.

On the Japanese side, motives of economic and political rivalry with the United States were linked to other, hidden, fears. For Japan, the close association with the United States since the war was a novel phenomenon. The traditional American posture towards Japan had been one of suspicion and rivalry. The United States had viewed the Anglo-Japanese alliance with distrust and had contributed to its termination.[27] The US had opposed Japan's advance in China since the beginning of the century. Was the Kissinger-Nixon initiative a return to the earlier East Asian policy of backing China against Japan? In addition, there was the psychological factor. Japan, the good pupil, emulated and eventually outdid the master. It had learnt the management of economic growth better than its Western advocates. Over the issue of dollar conversion in Okinawa, it had imitated very well the American practice of lack of consultation. Now it was to go further in the establishment of direct relations with Peking. All this was satisfying to national self-esteem.

One last observation may be useful at this point. In noting the developments leading up to and including the negotiations, one is struck by an emphasis, particularly on the Chinese side, on the acceptance of broad principles as a precondition for the opening of talks. We shall observe a similar phenomenon in negotiations after 1972. This has both a symbolic and a practical purpose, being a form of moral one-upmanship and a way of establishing one's bargaining position. Once your partner concedes a certain principle, say over territorial claims, you can afford to be generous over the details of an agreement although the concession may be exploited to his embarrassment in future negotiations on other matters. The choice of general and often vague language leaves plenty of room for fresh interpretations, as circumstances are always changing. The practical consequence of such an approach is a seemingly interminable wrangle over general principles, which, once it is resolved, may be followed by the rapid conclusion of the detailed negotiations on a particular issue.

Under such conditions, negotiations become an endurance test which it is difficult for the government of an open and pluralistic democracy to sustain. A large part of the explanation for Japanese behaviour in such situations must be sought in domestic pressures, in the processes by which decisions are reached, and in perceptions of the national interest. But some explanation may also be found in the difficulty they have of accepting the moral superiority so often implied in the Chinese insistence on the *principe préalable*.

THE DEVELOPMENT OF POLICY 1972–1976

The Chou-Tanaka communiqué referred, of course, to matters other than the status of Taiwan. China renounced any claim to reparations. It is interesting to speculate about the reasons for this gesture. China would certainly have benefited from an influx of Japanese technology and capital goods, and the state of the Japanese economy would not have made the payment of reparations unwelcome to Japanese business. It would have meant an opportunity to penetrate the Chinese economy with the support of government money, much as reparations had fuelled Japanese economic expansion into Southeast Asia in the 1950s and early 1960s. Perhaps it was precisely because of the danger of becoming too dependent, in certain sectors of the economy, on the Japanese that the Chinese waived their rights, although it is difficult to envisage how such a penetration could have taken place in the closely controlled Chinese economy. The Chinese may also have acted so magnanimously at Japanese urging that an agreement to pay reparations to China might have led to serious embarrassment with the Kuomintang; it would have been a kind of Chinese concession in return for Japan's 'understanding' of China's view of the Taiwan problem. But why should Peking have done anything to save Japan embarrassment in its relations with the Nationalist government? A more likely reason may have been an unwillingness on the part of the Chinese to appear less generous in 1972 than Chiang Kai-shek was in 1952 – it would not do to shine less in virtue, and, incidentally, to risk incurring ill-will among the Japanese by appearing to be vindictive.

Both countries also agreed to negotiate a treaty of peace and friendship, as well as agreements on trade, navigation, aviation, fisheries, etc. The course of relations with China has subsequently turned around the search for agreement over these issues. Finally, and, as it turned out, most important, both countries agreed not to seek hegemony in the Asia-Pacific region and each expressed opposition to any other country or group of countries which entertained such ambitions.

Quickest progress was made in the field of trade. The last Memorandum Trade Agreement was signed in November 1972, after only a few days of talks and with no political message attached to it. On 5 December 1972 a Japan-China Economic Association was inaugurated to organize the trade between the two countries with the object of planning for its expansion and keeping order among the Japanese competitors. Although a private organization, it was subsidized by the government. Early in 1973, Kokubōsoku announced the end of the 'Friendly Firms' system. The government for its part removed all restrictions on credit financing through the Export-Import Bank. From now on, trade between the two countries increased by leaps and bounds. A three-year trade pact was initialled in Peking at the end of 1973 and signed on 6 January 1974. It covered a whole range of matters from import duties to technological exchanges but it did not provide for non-discrimination. In other words, the restrictions imposed by COCOM still stood. The treaty also provided for the establishment of an official joint committee. The volume of the two-way trade tripled from $1100 million in 1972 to nearly $3300 million in 1974. Steel products and machinery registered striking advances. However, the main interest centred on the potential for crude oil imports from China.

Japan's trade with Taiwan suffered only a brief setback after the reversal of diplomatic relations. The Kuomintang had taken some measures of reprisal against Japan's 'perfidy', but they were not kept up for long and by the spring of 1973 restrictions on the import of plants and machinery from Japan had been lifted to a large extent. Economic interests were stronger than the growls and threats of the Nationalist leaders.

Trade had been resumed one month after the publication of the Chou-Tanaka communiqué. In January 1973 the Taiwanese opened a Tokyo branch office of the newly formed Association of East Asian Relations. The Japanese opened offices of the Private Interchange Association in Taipei and Kaohsiung. The missions of both countries were mainly staffed by diplomats on leave of absence. Soon major Japanese concerns were developing new ties with Taiwanese subsidiaries.

Japan seemed to be well on the way to a successful separation of economics from politics (Japanese style). For China it may have raised the spectre of a Japanese switch from a two Chinas policy to a 'separate Taiwan from China' policy. However, apart from a tendency to make haste slowly on some issues as they affect relations with China, there is no evidence to suggest that a policy of separating Taiwan from China has been adopted by the Japanese.

The Kuomintang (KMT) régime had by no means lost all its influence and importance in Japanese politics. Through its supporters in the government and the LDP it could seriously impede progress in the negotiations on specific issues between Peking and Tokyo. For, in order to gain the support of the pro-KMT elements in his party for the normalization of relations with the People's Republic, Tanaka had to promise that it would have only a minimal effect on relations with Taiwan.[28]

The difficulty of reconciling the demands of Peking with the interests of Taiwan and appeasing their respective supporters in Japan goes far to explain the long-protracted negotiations for a civil-aviation agreement. Several other reasons must also be taken into account and the whole exceedingly complex story has been ably recounted elsewhere.[29] Very significant in all this was Chinese willingness to tolerate, or at least turn a blind eye to, the existence of 'private' air links between Japan and Taiwan. What could not be tolerated was any hint that the Japanese regarded Taiwan as a sovereign entity. Foreign Minister Ōhira was willing to accept the Chinese position, but the deliberate leak of a draft statement to that effect was designed to weaken his position within the LDP, the majority of whose members were sympathetic to Taiwan.[30]

Agreement was eventually reached in time for inaugural flights between Japan and China to mark the second anniversary of the normalization of relations. A three-year Fisheries Pact in August 1975 presented fewer difficulties and those more of a technical nature, though the issue of Chinese territorial rights in the East China Sea loomed large.

The negotiations for a peace and friendship treaty began in January 1975 and ran into very rough weather; at the time of writing they remain unresolved. On 16 January 1975 preliminary talks were opened at the Gaimushō. Two sets of difficulties had to be overcome. One was raised at official level, the other stemmed from the pressures of the pro-Taiwan wing of the LDP.

Some officials of the Foreign Ministry pressed for a Chinese renunciation of the hostility directed against Japan in the preamble and first article of the 1950 Sino-Soviet Treaty of Friendship and Alliance. That treaty remains in effect until 1980. Others maintained that it had become a dead letter and suggested that a clarifying statement from the Chinese side would suffice. The Chinese presented a problem from their side by demanding the inclusion of Article (7), the celebrated anti-hegemony clause, of the Chou-Tanaka communiqué in the treaty. The Japanese demurred as this was a move directed against the Soviet Union. On the other hand, the Chinese side intimated that it would not raise the questions of Taiwan and territorial issues, as these had been 'settled' with the normalization of relations in 1972.

If the Chinese were accommodating over Taiwan, some members of the LDP were not. They wanted the word 'peace' omitted from the name of the treaty on the grounds that Japan had already concluded a peace treaty with the Nationalist Republic of China. They also demanded that the air route between Tokyo and Taipei should be reopened before the treaty was signed. On the first point the Chinese were willing to meet Japan's predicament by agreeing that it would not be a peace (*heiwa*) pact, ending a state of war, but an agreement which would govern relations of lasting peace and friendship (*wahei*). The activities of the pro-Taiwan lobby had an inhibiting effect on the government. Mr Miki, who had succeeded Mr Tanaka as premier, and his foreign minister had hoped to submit the treaty for ratification to the Diet before May 1975. As the negotiations continued it became obvious that the timetable would not be met.

An example of the delicate balancing which had to be used was the composition of Mr Hori's special mission to Peking on 15 January 1975. He went ostensibly to take a message from the new Japanese prime minister. The Chinese had invited him, which was in itself interesting as he had been closely associated with the unacceptable Mr Satō, though he himself had maintained a moderate position in the controversies over China. His hosts obviously wanted to inform themselves about the state of mind of the new administration in Tokyo – a government headed by a man with sympathies for China, backed by a party in which at least three key posts were held by men with avowed sympathies for Taiwan.

Hori's entourage included Tagawa Seiichi, a disciple of Matsumura Kenzō and a friend of the People's Republic. It also included Tsubokawa Shinzō, Chairman of the LDP's Public Relations Committee, a friend of the régime in Taiwan, which he had visited after the normalization of relations with Peking. Both elements of the LDP were thus discomfited. The pro-Taiwan wing was to some extent compromised by its participation in the mission. The pro-Peking group could hardly be enthusiastic that others were muscling in on a preserve which they had regarded as exclusively their own.

The negotiations over the peace and friendship treaty have dragged on and on in a plethora of statements and commentaries. The bargaining positions of both sides have focused on the anti-hegemony issue with its direct bearing on the Japanese-Sino-Soviet triangular relationship, which has become a major consideration in the formulation of Japanese policy towards China. It is necessary, therefore, to devote some attention to the evolution of this triangular diplomacy.

The Sino-Soviet-Japanese triangle has had a latent existence as a diplomatic sub-system since the beginning of the Sino-Soviet rift, but it was obscured by the implications of Sino-American hostility. It became an important feature in Japan's external relations as a result of Chinese and Russian attitudes to Japan, which emerged out of the interplay that started with the Sino-American *rapprochement*.

The story began with the opening of American-Vietnamese negotiations in 1969. The Americans, guided by Dr Kissinger's concert of powers diplomacy, started their moves towards China. The Chinese encouraged them discreetly while the Russians stepped up their support for Hanoi, both to make the *rapprochement* more difficult and to strengthen their own position in Southeast Asia *vis-à-vis* the Chinese. At first, the Chinese appeared to regard Japan as little else than a particularly vicious stooge of the United States. Publicly they continued their hostile stand towards the United States, but their greatest vituperation was reserved for Mr Satō and Japanese 'militarism'.

Russian reactions to the Sino-American détente and the impending change of leadership in the LDP, following the conclusion of the Okinawa Reversion Agreement on 17 June 1971, increased Chinese eagerness to see a successor to Mr Satō more favourable to themselves and to hasten the normalization of relations between the two countries in order to forestall Russian moves to counter the Sino-American *rapprochement* with closer Soviet-Japanese ties. In the rivalry for the succession to the presidency of the LDP, Mr Tanaka was believed to prefer an early establishment of relations with China, while Mr Fukuda was reported to favour a more cautious approach and giving priority to the improvement of relations with Russia. However, taking into account the constraints of domestic politics and the national mood, it is doubtful whether it would have made much difference to policy who became prime minister.

This is the background to the series of diplomatic manœuvres which began in late 1971 and have continued to the time of writing. Whenever one of the communist powers made a move towards Japan, the other has tried to match it and neutralize the effect. Each power combined warnings and threats over Japanese approaches to the other with hints and promises of favours to come if the Japanese behaved themselves.

From 23 to 27 January 1972 – on the eve of President Nixon's visit to China – Mr Gromyko was in Tokyo. The communiqué published at the end of his stay announced an agreement to open negotiations for a peace treaty within the year. There were renewed reports of Russian flexibility over the Northern Territories issue and a suggestion that the Soviet position was once more that of 1956.[31] The Russians had also made a number of specific promises and gestures pleasing to the Japanese. All this evoked a sour reaction from Peking which castigated the 'collaboration' between 'Soviet revisionist social-imperialism' and the 'Japanese reactionaries' and supported 'the Japanese people's demands' for the return of the Northern Territories.[32]

Immediately after Mr Tanaka became prime minister in July 1972 the Russian attitude cooled perceptibly. Originally it had been hoped that negotiations for a peace settlement would begin in September, but by the middle of that month there was still no mention of a date and Japanese inquiries prove fruitless. The ambassador in Moscow was unable to see Mr Gromyko or any of his assistants.

Yet, shortly after Mr Tanaka's return from Peking, the Russian ambassador gave him a personal message from Mr Brezhnev, expressing the hope that a peace treaty would be concluded shortly. When Foreign Minister Ōhira arrived in Moscow a week later the Russians were willing to discuss the Northern Territories, although they were very reserved over their position. It was then assumed that no serious negotiations would start before the spring of 1973. Mr Tanaka hardened the Japanese position after Mr Ōhira's return. He told a press conference on 26 October 1972 that the return of the four northern islands was essential for the conclusion of a peace treaty.

The Chinese in the meanwhile did everything they could to exacerbate the territorial issue. At the beginning of August 1972 Mr Chou told the president of Kōmeitō, a close friend of Mr Tanaka, that China supported Japan's claim to the southern Kurile Islands. At the end of the year it was reported, but denied by official spokesmen in Tokyo, that, at his meeting with Mr Tanaka, the Chinese premier had raised the possibility of Chinese troops fighting alongside the Japanese to repel a Russian attack on Japan.

Early in 1973 the complicated dance between the three states continued. After the Soviet ambassador in Japan had called for new methods to resume negotiations over a peace treaty, Mr Tanaka omitted mention of the territorial claim in a general policy speech before the Diet in January 1973, the first time that this had been done in fifteen years. Almost immediately, Chou En-lai pointedly offered China's full support to Japan over the territorial issue. He also told another of Mr Tanaka's friends, Kimura Takeo, LDP Diet member and former Minister, that the Mutual Security Treaty with the United States was a necessary protection against the Soviet Union.

At the end of February Mr Tanaka made known his desire to visit Moscow in the second half of 1973. On 13 March the Japanese ambassador handed over a personal message from the Japanese premier to Mr Brezhnev, with whom he had a 'warm' talk for two and a half hours. Peking's reaction was quick to come. Again it was double-edged. The Chinese for the first time publicly denounced possible Japanese-Soviet co-operation in developing the Tyumen oil field in western Siberia. They also announced the forthcoming visit of an important mission to Japan. Nothing daunted, Mr Nakasone assured the Soviet ambassador two days later of Japanese government support for the Siberian development projects, with the promise of large credits from the Export-Import Bank. However, by the summer of 1973 a new frigidity had entered Soviet-Japanese relations.

The reasons for the change in attitude are obscure. They may have been related to the high-level mission from the China-Japan Friendship Association, headed by Liao Cheng-chih, which spent a month in Japan from April to May. Probably more important was the break-through in negotiations for the Sino-Japanese Trade Agreement, which was initialled in December 1973, and the increased volume of Sino-Japanese economic relations. There were also reports of China's interest in Japanese participation in the development of the oil resources in the Gulf of Po Hai.

These developments must be set against the background of deteriorating relations between Russia and China and speculations about a Soviet military attack on China. The deepening leadership crisis in China was also thought to offer opportunities for some form of Russian intervention.

When Mr Tanaka went to Moscow on his way back from Europe in October 1973 there was complete impasse in Japanese-Soviet relations and he returned empty-handed. For the Japanese, the principal objective was to set up negotiations for a peace treaty. The Russians wanted Japan to accept the Soviet view of the situation in east Asia, which meant falling in with the idea of an Asian collective security system. The objective behind Mr Brezhnev's plan was to gain acceptance of the existing frontiers in Asia and to establish a network of agreements which would effectively isolate China. This ran counter to Japanese policy which was to maintain the existing security arrangements, meaning the Mutual Security Treaty with the United States, and to make sure that any future agreements would include China and the US. The basic Japanese idea was that the best way to stabilize the Asian-Pacific region was through a four-power agreement. Most important, of course, was Japan's refusal to countenance any 'freezing' of frontiers as long as the territorial issue had not been settled.

In the spring of 1974 the endless discussions about Japanese participation in the development of Siberia took a new turn, with Soviet proposals for the construction of a second Siberian railway to replace part of the projected pipeline for the transport of oil from the Tyumen field to the Pacific coast. The railway was to run from Tayshet, northwest of Irkutsk, near Lake Baikal, to a port for shipment to Japan.

The financial and strategic implications were obvious and the Japanese expressed their reservations. The Soviet side then modified the proposal. It was suggested that the railway would run only to Khabarovsk, from where oil would be moved through a pipeline. The Japanese were assured that the railway project was not part of a package deal but that it would be handled separately from the five other major joint projects under consideration. Russian spokesmen insisted that it would be built without foreign help, although part of the proposed Japanese loan for the development of Tyumen oil might be used to buy equipment for the railway.

The renewed exchanges with Japan at the highest level (Mr Kosygin went to Moscow International Airport on 5 April 1974 to meet Mr Tanaka, who was on his way to Paris to attend the memorial service for President Pompidou) and the more encouraging Russian tone coincided with the climax in the negotiations with China over a civil aviation agreement.

A month after the signature of that agreement the Soviet tone became colder. At a press conference on 28 May 1974 the Soviet minister in charge of the oil industry said that Russia needed no foreign help in the development of Siberia. He denied that there had been any serious negotiations with the Japanese over the exploitation of the Tyumen field and implied that the only area in which the Russians would consider a joint venture was in the exploration for oil off the coast of Sakhalin. As for the projected railway, he remarked : 'You can only send oil through a pipeline, but by rail you can ship anything you want.'

Nevertheless, other developments pointed to a renewed warming of Japanese-Soviet relations. A memorandum on the joint development of coking coal in southern Yakutsk was signed in early May. This was the first draft agreement to be concluded on any of the long-projected joint ventures for the development of Siberia. It was also reported that one Japanese objective in hastening the conclusion of the civil aviation agreement had been to 'encourage' a more forthcoming attitude from the Russians.

Tanaka was to be disappointed. He was forced to resign without having made any further progress. As soon as Mr Miki was installed as his successor, at the end of 1974, there was a burst of diplomatic activity, the ground for which had been partly prepared under Tanaka. On 15 January 1975 Foreign Minister Miyazawa went to Moscow. On the same day Mr Hori went to Peking. On 16 January Mr Miyazawa and Mr Gromyko held the first of three sessions in Moscow to examine the prospects for a peace treaty. Again, on the same day, preliminary talks on the projected Sino-Japanese treaty of peace and friendship opened at the Gaimushō in Tokyo.

In this latest manifestation of Sino-Soviet rivalry over Japan, the Chinese seemed to be making greater headway, although there were difficulties in the positions of all three parties. A ray of hope appeared in Moscow that there might be progress in Soviet-Japanese relations because Mr Gromyko did not insist that the territorial question had been settled, when replying to Japanese demands that it had to be settled before they could sign a peace treaty. However, the Japanese side rejected a Soviet proposal for a treaty of friendship and goodwill, which had been advanced by Gromyko and was similar to the suggestion of 'intermediate' means made by Mr Kosygin in 1967, being largely designed to circumvent the territorial question.

In their dialogue with the Chinese, the Japanese were just as anxious to avoid taking an anti-Soviet stand as they were to avoid taking an anti-Chinese stand in negotiations with the Russians. The Chinese wanted to include the wording of Article (7) of the Chou-Tanaka communiqué in the projected treaty : 'Neither of the two countries should seek hegemony in the Asia-Pacific region and each country is opposed to efforts by any other country or group of countries to establish such hegemony.' There could be no fundamental objection to the first part of this statement, but the second part might have appeared to be too obviously directed against the Soviet Union, particularly in view of the partial American withdrawal from Asia and Chinese approval of the US-Japan Mutual Security Treaty. It is believed that Peking wanted to include some stipulation that the two parties would consult each other if any third power tried to establish a hegemony in the region. The inclusion of such a provision would, in the view of the Japanese Foreign Ministry, have been tantamount to establishing a Sino-Japanese alliance and was, therefore, totally unacceptable.[33]

It must be remembered that the inclusion of the anti-hegemony clause was strenuously opposed by all those in the ruling circles of Japan who wanted to avoid any point that might alienate the Soviet Union. They did everything they could to stress the anti-Soviet intent behind the Chinese position over the issue. As a result, the official Japanese policy was interpreted as not wanting to offend Russia in order to gain the friendship of China. This could only have had the effect of hardening the Chinese position.

In early 1975 Sino-Japanese relations had become nicely stuck over the problem of where and in what sense to include the opposition to hegemony in the treaty. By the end of the year, the Japanese position on the issue was crystallized in what came to be known as 'the four principles', enunciated by Foreign Minister Miyazawa. They were : (1) the opposition to hegemony was in no sense directed against a specific third country; (2) it did not imply joint Sino-Japanese action against any state which might seek hegemony in the region; (3) it applied to all parts of the world; (4) it conformed to the Charter of the United Nations. China's acceptance of these principles was a precondition for Japan's readiness to incorporate a declaration of opposition to hegemony in the treaty. The question of whether it should be in the preamble or in the main text was considered to be a 'technical' matter.[34]

There was no substantial progress in the negotiations throughout 1976. Moreover, the entanglement of Japan's relations with China and Russia was once again demonstrated in July, when Mr Miyazawa complained that China's support over the territorial dispute with the Soviet Union was unhelpful and the Foreign Ministry asked the

Chinese to refrain from interfering in what was a purely bilateral issue. This earned him the praise of Tass and a severe rebuke from *The People's Daily*.[35]

When Mr Kosaka Zentarō succeeded Mr Miyazawa at the Foreign Ministry on 15 September 1976, it seemed likely that he would take new initiatives over the treaty and not feel bound by Miyazawa's 'principles'.[36] However, by this time both China and Japan were in the throes of domestic political crises which made a major break-through in negotiations impossible. On 24 December 1976, after an election in which the LDP almost lost control of the House of Representatives, Mr Fukuda replaced Mr Miki as prime minister and Mr Kosaka was out of office.

CONCLUSION

The course of Japanese policy towards China since 1972 has shown that the issues which played such an important part in the bilateral relationship were by no means eliminated by the normalization of relations. Trade grew in importance, with oil as a new factor in it, but it acquired some independence of the political issues. The influence of Taiwan remained a factor in domestic politics but it was no longer the chief obstacle to the development of political relations with China. Japan's 'unofficial' relations with Taiwan were the means with which the pro-Taiwan elements could make relations with Peking more difficult – by provoking Chinese reactions which would embarrass the government. Finally, security became a problem which embraced more than the Japanese-American alliance and its implications for Taiwan.

New problems arose which overshadowed or transformed the earlier issues. The most important was the issue of how best to manage relations with the Soviet Union and China, which became a matter of central importance for Japan's diplomacy and security. In domestic politics this question took the place of the previous argument over China versus Taiwan.

NOTES

1 Utsunomiya Tokuma, a prominent member of the LDP with strong sympathies for the People's Republic of China, reported in the *Shūkan Post* of 5 Feb 1971, that on a visit to the US in Jan 1971 he had heard of secret preparations by Henry Kissinger for the recognition of Peking. See 'America Has Already Completed Preparations for Recognizing China', Translation Service, American Embassy, Tokyo, *Summaries of Selected Japanese Magazines*, Feb 1971, pp. 43–7.

2   After this incident Satō was reported to have told the journalists on duty at his residence that 'it feels good to make a decision by jumping over the head [of the US].' *Yomiuri*, 10 Oct 1971.
3   Text of the communiqué of the Trade Memorandum Agreement, signed in Peking, 1 Mar 1971. *NHNA*, 1 Mar 1971.
4   *Mainichi Daily News*, 26 Aug 1971; *JT*, 6 Oct 1971.
5   *JT*, 25 July 1971.
6   *JT*, 15 Oct 1971.
7   '. . . our most formidable rivals in prospective trade with People's China are the three American giants.' Katō Seishi, Vice-President of Toyota Motor Sales, *Mainichi Daily News*, 9 Sep 1971.
8   *JT*, 11 Sep 1971. See also above, p. 26.
9   This was especially so in the contest for the presidency of the LDP and during the formation of a new cabinet. A prospective prime minister might be forced to moderate particular policies in order to buy the support of influential faction leaders.
10 *Yomiuri*, 10 Oct 1971; *JT*, 15 Oct 1971.
11 Fujiyama was a businessman and a close associate of Kishi. This did not stop him from promoting a campaign for improved relations with the PRC. He had always been sympathetic to China. In 1971 he played a leading part in mobilizing all-party support for the normalization of relations. Some observers saw this as a bid for political power, especially as it was thought that the LDP might break up over the China issue.
12 Ikeda had been Director of the Diet Members' League for the Promotion of Sino-Japanese Trade, founded in 1949, which agitated for the relaxation of the embargo under COCOM.
13 Kaya was the leader of the pro-Taiwan 'Asian Group' of the LDP. However, he had been open-minded about trade with the Mainland.
14 Nakao was identified with the pro-Taiwan lobby. A member of the Nakasone faction, he later joined the right-wing *Seirankai* (Blue Storm Society) of young turks in the Party.
15 *Mainichi Daily News*, 17 July 1971.
16 Watanuki J., Okabe K., and Miyajima T., 'International Attitudes and Party Support of the Japanese People', *Peace Research in Japan: 1968* (Tokyo, The Japan Peace Research Group), pp. 5–6.
17 *Le Monde*, 15 Jan 1972.
18 Cited in Etō Shinkichi, 'Japan and China – a New Stage?', *Problems of Communism* (Washington, US Information Agency), vol. XXI, no. 6, Nov–Dec 1972, pp. 7 and 9.
19 *JT*, 7 Mar 1972.
20 *NHNA*, 2 July 1971. Kōmeitō did not, however, accept the Chinese position unconditionally in every respect. I was told by a source close to the Kōmeitō delegation that the Chinese pressed their views vigorously, but the tactics of Takeiri Yoshikatsu, leader of the delegation, who threatened at one stage to break off the discussions and return home, led to some flexibility in the Chinese position. The text of the communiqué did not attack Prime Minister Satō directly.
21 *JT*, 30 Sep 1972.

22 Ibid., 1 Oct 1972.
23 Ibid., 1 Nov 1972.
24 Etō, p. 12.
25 Ibid., p. 11. For a discussion of the historic tribute system, see Mark Mancall, 'The Ch'ing Tribute System: an Interpretative Essay', in J. K. Fairbank, ed., *The Chinese World Order: Traditional China's Foreign Relations* (Cambridge, Mass., Harvard UP, 1968). Also, M. F. Nelson, *Korea and the Old Orders in Eastern Asia* (Baton Rouge, Louisiana State Univ. Press, 1946), p. 18.
26 Takeiri Yoshikatsu was not only the Chairman of Kōmeitō but also a personal friend of Mr Tanaka. In 1969 the latter had tried to come to the rescue of Kōmeitō, which had been accused of trying to suppress the controversial book by Fujiwara Hirotatsu, *Sōka Gakkai o Kiru,* translated into English by Worth C. Grant, under the title *I Denounce Sōka Gakkai* (Tokyo, Nisshin Hōdō Co., 1970). Three years later Mr Takeiri was able to repay the obligation by acting as go-between for Mr Tanaka with the Chinese and was reported to have transmitted a secret document from them to the Japanese Premier in Aug 1972. *The Times,* 14 Sep 1972; *Le Monde,* 14 Sep 1972.
27 For a discussion of American attitudes and policies towards the Anglo-Japanese alliance, see the second volume of Ian Nish's study of that alliance, *Alliance in Decline: a Study in Anglo-Japanese Relations 1908–1922* (London, The Athlone Press, 1972).
28 J. W. M. Chapman, 'Britain, Japan and the China Aviation Tangle, 1974–1976', in Peter Lowe, ed., *Proceedings of the British Association for Japanese Studies,* vol. I, pt. 1: *History and International Relations* (Centre of Japanese Studies, Univ. of Sheffield, 1976), p. 174.
29 Ibid., *passim.*
30 The information was made public by two members of the LDP's Japan-Taiwan Dietmen's Council. The statement included the following passage: 'The Japan-China Civil Aviation Agreement is an agreement between the two countries while the Japan-Taiwan flights are a regional, private air service. The Japanese Government has not recognized the markings on the Taiwanese aircraft as the so-called national flag since the Japan-China joint communiqué was issued. Nor has the Government regarded the CAL as a flag carrier of any state.' See *Mainichi Daily News,* 11 and 12 Apr 1974. CAL refers of course to China Airlines (Nationalist).
31 The four Northern Territories in question are a small group of islands known as the Habomais and a larger island, Shikotan, lying off the Nemuro peninsula of Hokkaidō, which the Japanese regard as an extension of that island and the Russians call the 'Little Kuriles', and the two southernmost islands of the Kurile chain, Kunashiri and Etorofu (Kunashir and Iturup in Russian).
     The history of the Japanese-Russian encounter in this region is very complex. Both countries dispute the right to ownership of the Kuriles on historical grounds. In negotiations preceding the Treaty of Shimoda of 1855, the Russians laid claim to Etorofu but not to the other islands. By the terms of the Treaty, all the four Northern Territories were

recognized as Japanese. In 1875, by the Treaty of St Petersburg, the Japanese acquired the rest of the Kurile chain northwards to Kamchatka peninsula in return for ceding their rights in Sakhalin. They took Southern Sakhalin in 1905 by the Treaty of Portsmouth which ended the Russo-Japanese War.

At Yalta, in Feb 1945, Roosevelt agreed that Southern Sakhalin and the Kuriles should pass to Russia in return for a promise to enter the war against Japan after Germany's surrender. The Russians occupied Southern Sakhalin, Etorofu, Kunashiri, the Habomais, and Shikotan at the end of the war and incorporated Sakhalin and the Kuriles into the Soviet Union. In Chapter II, Article 2(c) of the Treaty of San Francisco, Japan renounced all rights and claims to Southern Sakhalin and the Kuriles but the treaty did not specify to whom they were to belong.

The Joint Declaration of 1956, which re-established diplomatic relations between Russia and Japan, stipulated in Article 9 that the Habomais and Shikotan should be returned to Japan on conclusion of a peace treaty between the two countries but made no mention of the other territories. It had seemed as if the Japanese government would be content to settle for the islands off Nemuro, but pressures within the LDP, arising from the exigencies of factional politics, and an American intervention during the course of the Japanese-Soviet negotiations, made it harden its position to include claims on Etorofu and Kunashiri. Since the Japanese changed their position in the middle of negotiations, there was no prospect of signing the hoped-for peace treaty, which had been the original intention.

Ever since 1956 the argument has turned round the interpretation of the Allied wartime agreements, the San Francisco Treaty, and the Declaration of 1956. In 1960 the Russians added the stipulation that no territories would be returned until all American troops had been withdrawn from Japan.

So far, the issue seems insoluble as the Japanese insist on the return of all four territories while the Soviet Union oscillates between refusal to consider any claim and hints that it might be prepared to negotiate over the Habomais and Shikotan. The territories have considerable strategic importance and are situated in major fishing grounds.

The most comprehensive treatment of the whole issue is to be found in John J. Stephan, *The Kuril Islands: Russo-Japanese Frontier in the Pacific* (Oxford, Clarendon Press, 1974). See also *The Northern Islands* (Public Information Bureau, Ministry of Foreign Affairs of Japan, 1955); E. O. Reischauer, *The United States and Japan*, 3rd edn (New York, Viking Press, 1972), pp. 239–41; J. L. Sutton, 'Territorial Claims of Russia and Japan in the Kurile Islands', *Occasional Papers*, no. 1 (Univ. of Michigan Press, Ann Arbor, 1951), pp. 34–61; E. Pond, 'Japan and Russia: the View from Tokyo', *Foreign Affairs*, Oct 1973, pp. 141–52; *Wall Street Journal*, 16 May 1969; *JT*, 28 Oct 1971; Shimizu Takehisa, 'Northern Territories Issue – Refuting the Hirasawa Thesis', and Sase Masamori, 'The Northern Territories in International Politics', *Japan Echo*, vol. III, no. 2, Summer 1976, pp. 45–66.

32 *Peking Review*, 11 Feb 1972. In the 1950s the Chinese supported the Soviet Union over the Kuriles. The first intimation of a change in the Chinese position came from Mao Tse-tung in 1964, when he told a JSP delegation that the Kuriles should be returned to Japan. Stephan, pp. 221–2.

33 There is an interesting historical parallel here illustrating Japan's reluctance to enter into any agreement which might be construed as a Sino-Japanese alliance. During the negotiations for the Treaty of Friendship in 1871, the Japanese side at first resisted the inclusion of Article 2, which had been proposed by China. The article stipulated that: '. . . it is the duty of each to sympathize with the other, and in the event of any other nation acting unjustly or treating either of two Powers with contempt, on notice being given [by the one to the other], mutual assistance shall be rendered, or mediation offered for the arrangement of the difficulty, in fulfilment of the duty imposed by relations of friendship.'

As in the case of the 'anti-hegemony' issue a hundred years later, the Japanese government feared in 1871 that third parties would interpret this as a treaty of alliance. The fears were borne out for, after Japan had accepted the article, a number of states (including the US but not Russia) accused it of having entered into an alliance with China. I am indebted to Professor Dore for drawing my attention to this and to Mr Ninomiya Saburō of the National Diet Library for supplying me with information. An English text of the treaty may be found in Sir Edward Hertslet, *Treaties, etc., between Great Britain and China; and between China and Foreign Powers; and Orders in Council, Rules, Regulations, Acts of Parliament, Decrees and Notifications affecting British Interests in China*, vol. I, (London, Harrison, 1896), p. 241.

34 *JTW*, 15 Nov 1975.

35 Ibid., 17 July 1976; *The Guardian*, 20 July 1976; *The International Herald Tribune*, 21 July 1976.

36 Mr Kosaka had the reputation of being something of a Sinophil. He had been Foreign Minister in the early years of the Ikeda cabinet, from 1960 to 1962, and had paid four visits to China in the postwar period, the latest having been in 1975. He had good contacts among the Chinese leaders and on taking office had expressed his determination to press for a prompt resumption of the stalled negotiations. Moreover, he did not feel bound by a rigid adherence to Mr Miyazawa's 'four principles'. It is noteworthy that whereas Mr Miyazawa was a bureaucrat (Finance Ministry) turned politician, Mr Kosaka was a businessman turned politician. However, a change of policy was not the reason why Mr Miki changed his foreign minister. In spite of having belonged to one of the anti-Miki factions in the LDP, Mr Kosaka refused to join the movement to oust the Prime Minister in the leadership crisis of 1976. Mr Miyazawa, on the other hand, had given some support to the anti-Miki forces. *JTW*, 25 Sep and 30 Oct 1976; *The Guardian*, 16 Sep 1976.

4 Aspects of the China Problem in the Late 1970s

IT was noted in the previous chapter that the diplomatic normalization of inter-state relations did not automatically remove the issues which had dominated the China problem since the early Fifties. However, changes in their context, their content, and their relative importance have made some redefinition of the analytical framework desirable. Now, therefore, I propose to consider the contemporary problems of Japan's relations with China, and shall do so under four headings: economic and commercial relations; bilateral political issues; China in Japan's relations with third countries; China in domestic politics.

ECONOMIC AND COMMERCIAL RELATIONS

Before the Pacific War, Japan's economy depended heavily on the East and Southeast Asian regions, particularly Manchuria and China. Since the war, Japan's economy has come to depend on the global economy. China remains an important factor in the formulation of economic policy, but it is only one among a number of important factors and of less weight than some others.

The greatest single factor is the economic relationship with the United States. Although the value of trade with the US, on a customs clearance basis, has fallen from 29 per cent (1968) to 21 per cent (1976) of Japan's total foreign trade, the relationship extends much further than the annual balance sheet of visible trade. The United States accounts for 60 per cent of Japan's imports of the coking coal essential for steel production, which provides such a significant proportion of Japan's exports to China. It is the sole source of enriched uranium for Japan's nuclear industry, and one of the major suppliers of animal feedstuffs. American companies are the principal suppliers of Japan's oil. Much of the iron ore and coke imported from Australia is mined by American companies.[1]

The shift in economic relations from China to the United States was the dominant characteristic in the 1950s and 1960s, but even before the end of the last decade, a new shift in Japan's economic relations became noticeable. Partly the result of strains in the bilateral relationship with the United States, it received a major impetus from the international oil crisis of 1973–4 and that whole complex of developments which includes the rising cost of primary products, domestic inflation, the international trade recession, and so on.

Apart from some decline in Japan's growth rate and in the total volume of foreign trade – which may well turn out to be short-term phenomena – we are probably at the beginning of a more lasting change in the pattern of Japan's foreign trade.

Between 1968 and 1976 the proportion of trade with the United States in relation to trade with the developed world as a whole declined from more than one half to less than one half in value. The proportion of trade with western Europe, on the other hand, has increased steadily. The two-way trade with Southeast Asia has also shown a tendency to decline in relation to trade with the developing areas of the world. The enormous jump in the value of trade with those areas since 1974 reflects the impact of the high prices of oil and other natural resources. This is particularly noticeable in the huge deficits which Japan has mounted in its trade with the Middle East (see Table V, below). The evidence points generally to a further spread of Japan's trading interests, caused by both the indefatigable search for sources of raw materials and the growing resistance of the North American and West European markets to Japanese goods.

Commerce with the communist countries, including China, has grown in volume over the years, but in 1976 it still remained a very small fraction of total exports and imports. Nor are there any indications that it will increase to a substantially greater proportion of total trade in the next few years.

Another development, which promises important consequences, has been the rapid increase in Japan's overseas investments. Though still lagging far behind the United States and Britain, Japan has joined West Germany among the four leading overseas investors in the world. Some of the funds are moving into manufacturing industries in South Korea, Taiwan, and the developed countries of Europe and North America, but the bulk of the investment is in resource-rich areas. On current trends, the main recipients (not necessarily in order of importance) of Japanese capital should be Australia, Brazil, Canada, Indonesia, Nigeria, Iran and other Middle Eastern countries.

The acquisition of a guaranteed supply of raw materials and sources of energy is a major concern of the economic planners. The government still vacillates between depending on bilateral agreements for this purpose, which would mean tying up Japanese capital and technology in

D

resource-rich countries in return for assured supplies, and the attractions of moving freely in world markets, buying where it is cheapest and most profitable. Bilateral arrangements seem of greater interest, partly because they facilitate long-term planning and stockpiling, but past experience with such agreements has not been altogether happy for Japan and its suppliers.[2]

These two current trends – the globalization of Japan's economic interests and the key importance of a national resources policy – are essential elements in the equation of Japan's trade with China. Without consideration of this wider background, a mere reading of trade statistics can be misleading.

So far as the value of Japanese trade with China is concerned, there has been an enormous advance. In 1974 it exceeded that with Taiwan for the first time since 1968. By 1975 it was nearly four times the value of four years earlier. Even when inflation is taken into account these are substantial advances. Other factors have strengthened the impression of significant growth. Industry's reliance on China as an export market has been increasing. Early in 1973, for instance, six major Japanese steel firms concluded an agreement worth $217 million with the China National Metals and Minerals Import and Export Corporation, which was believed to have been the largest of its kind ever concluded anywhere. By the beginning of 1976 China had become Japan's third largest export market. However, a rather different picture emerges when these facts are set against Japan's global trade. In that context, trade with China amounts to less than 3 per cent of Japan's total foreign trade.

Trade languished in 1976 and was 20 per cent below its value in the previous year and there were doubts whether it would recover fully in 1977. Several explanations were offered : political disturbances in China; slow recovery from the recession in Japan; the great imbalance in Japan's favour; disappointing Chinese exports; and so on. Of these, the trade imbalance seems the least convincing. The excess of Japanese exports over imports from China had been an annual feature of trade since 1972 and did not prevent an overall increase. The recession is only a partial explanation. At such times, Japanese industry has cast longing eyes on China as a result of shrinking markets at home and elsewhere. However, the most recent slump has affected Japanese consumption of oil, a commodity which has replaced textile materials as China's major export to Japan.

By the end of 1976 there was some improvement in Sino-Japanese trade, with a marked increase in Chinese imports, including the purchase of large computers from Hitachi, an order for steel at twice the amount contracted for in the spring, and so on. This movement appears to reflect a new emphasis on industrial development in China and not a substantial increase in Japanese purchases of oil.

The problems of the trade in oil and the uncertainties about China's economic policy have become, from Japan's point of view, the major issues in the bilateral economic relationship. They are not unrelated, for, technical considerations apart, the availability of Chinese oil depends on the politico-economic priorities of China's rulers.

The prospect of acquiring large quantities of Chinese oil is becoming something of the mirage that the prospects of the China trade turned out to be in the early postwar years. Chinese crude production jumped spectacularly from about 10 million tons in 1966 to an estimated 60 million tons by the end of 1974. Forecasts of production by the end of the decade and of the amounts available for export to Japan have varied widely. Some have suggested that Japan might import 100 million tons annually by 1980, one-third of its estimated requirements. Others have estimated annual imports of 30 million tons by that date (10 per cent of national requirements). The facts of the trade have told a very different story.

Until 1974 Japan bought negligible quantities of Chinese crude. In 1974 it imported 4 million tons (1·6 per cent of all imports of oil), which represented a cut of nearly 20 per cent in the amount contracted for. The figure was 8·1 million tons in 1975 and the outlook for 1976 is in the region of 6 to 8 million tons. There is no more talk of importing 100 million tons by 1980; not even of 30 million tons. Negotiations in early 1976 for a five-year contract were reported to include Japanese proposals for a target of 18 million tons by 1982. A Chinese official reduced expectations still further when he told a Keidanren delegation in April 1977 that China would be able to export 10 million tons of oil and 5 million tons of coal annually to Japan by 1982.[3]

In trying to foster the trade in oil, the Japanese face formidable difficulties. One of the most fundamental, which affects all commercial relations with China, is ignorance about China's economy; the Chinese authorities are reluctant to furnish information about it – and it is doubtful whether they themselves dispose of accurate statistics. Economists are, therefore, reduced to intelligent guesswork, which is not a very satisfactory basis on which to make long-term plans. The quality of Chinese oil, its price, and its competitive standing in relation to oil from the Middle East and Indonesia are other problems. Apparently the Japanese were not fully aware of the high wax content of Chinese oil when they first contracted to buy it in 1973. Moreover, the Chinese set a price per barrel which was nearly 1 dollar more than the cost of a barrel of Indonesian oil of comparable quality.[4]

In weighing up the arguments for and against efforts to increase their imports of Chinese oil, the Japanese must take a number of factors into account. First, there has been a steady decline in the expectations of the amount of oil the Chinese are able or willing to export. Then there is the question of how much to invest in setting up 'cracking' refineries in Japan to deal with the high wax content of Chinese oil, thereby becoming more dependent on it. Alternatively, Japan might help to finance the construction of refineries in China and assist in developing the infrastructure of communications, roads, ports, etc., which would strengthen China's capacity as an exporter. On the face of it there would be a considerable advantage in providing capital and technology in return for a guaranteed flow of oil at competitive prices. Such a dependence, however, raises the question of China's reliability as a source of oil. In this respect, the Japanese experience in negotiating with the Soviet Union over the development of the Tyumen field has not been very encouraging.[5]

One could continue with the catalogue of problems, and, no doubt, the Chinese have their difficulties with the Japanese. For example, they would like firmer Japanese commitments on the level of oil imports.[6] The technical and commercial difficulties between the two parties are no different in nature from those found in economic negotiations between any two countries. But behind them lurk peculiar political problems, which may render them particularly intractable.

For the Japanese, these may be summed up in the word 'uncertainty'; uncertainty about Chinese intentions, uncertainty about the Chinese economy, uncertainty about the economic priorities of the Chinese government, above all, uncertainty about the political scene in China. Basic to Japanese doubts is the fear that China will seek to exploit any economic advantage for political purposes. If Japan became very dependent on China for oil or other essential materials such as coal, China could threaten to cut off supplies at any time of tension between the two countries. The abrupt postponement, without explanation, of an official Chinese mission, which was to have gone to Japan in July 1976 to discuss shipping relations between the two countries, is a small example of how the Chinese might give expression to their anger over some Japanese action – in this case the remarks by Foreign Minister Miyazawa that Japan would not welcome a drastic change in Sino-American relations at the expense of the United States guarantee of Taiwan's security.[7]

The above example may be trivial but it illustrates the point. If the Chinese were prepared to show their displeasure in this way over a matter which both sides agreed not to pursue further,[8] then what would they be prepared to do over an issue which they regarded as far more serious? The obvious case here would be some concrete manifestation of Japanese-Soviet collaboration.

Both Russia and China are in a position to offer Japan essential sources of energy – if not immediately, then at least in the future. To develop their energy potential, both are in need of capital and technology, some of which Japan could provide, but whether it could simultaneously meet substantial demands from both countries is doubtful. Furthermore, Japan's experience of Chinese reactions to the proposals for the construction of a second Siberian railway will strengthen its caution over entering into any substantial deal with either country.

Japan's commercial intercourse with China therefore retains a political significance. However, that significance is no longer primarily in the area of the bilateral political relationship but in that of Japan's relations with third countries.

BILATERAL POLITICAL ISSUES

At the time of writing, the outstanding issue between the two countries is the signature of a treaty of peace and friendship. Premier Fukuda Takeo is not known for his enthusiasm for the People's Republic of China. His dependence on the support of pro-PRC elements in the LDP and the slender majority he commands in the Diet do not promise a major change in China policy. On the other hand, the political uncertainty in Japan, which was accentuated by the results of the elections to the House of Representatives at the end of 1976, must surely be one reason why the Chinese, for their part, do not appear to be more insistent, as they were a year or two previously. On the Japanese side, uncertainties about the course of Chinese policy after the deaths of Chou En-lai and Mao Tse-tung within the space of nine months undoubtedly strengthen the usual caution of the Foreign Ministry.

These considerations apart, the treaty issue raises several problems for Japan. The first concerns the best way in which to adjust to the Sino-Soviet conflict. If it were only the Russians who had made an issue out of the anti-hegemony clause, it would be up to the Japanese to decide how seriously to take Soviet protests and threats. In that case the solution might present a fairly clear-cut choice for Japanese diplomacy. However, there is a second problem of a more subtle kind. The form in which the anti-hegemony policy should be included in the treaty involves nuances of interpretation. Should it be a general statement in the preamble, or should it be one of the treaty clauses? Should Japan issue an explanatory statement disavowing any intent to form an alliance with China against third parties? These questions relate not only to the general problem of Japan's position in the confrontation between the Soviet Union and China but also bring in Japan's relationship with the United States.

Finally, Japan's status in relation to China is also involved. As the Japanese might see it, the anti-hegemony issue is a moral issue for China. Its acceptance has become a test of Japan's sincerity and good faith, which involves 'treading on Russia's face', just as in the sixteenth and seventeenth centuries Japanese Christians had been made to tread on a copper tablet of the crucifix to demonstrate their apostasy. A similar issue arises over Taiwan. Until such time as the People's Republic of China is able to assert its sovereignty over the island in a more concrete fashion, it must have formal acceptances of its rights over Taiwan. Hence, any hint of a deviation from such a recognition, as in Mr Miyazawa's comments about Sino-American relations, is immediately seized upon as an act of betrayal. In the Japanese perception, the Chinese probably distinguish between them, as members of the same racial and cultural family, and other outsiders, like the Americans, from whom one cannot expect as much. More is expected from a blood relation to prove his good faith.

The Japanese have always been divided over whether to bow to China's wishes in these matters and thus accept China's moralism or whether to resist it. The new-found national self-confidence of the 1960s and 1970s, as well as Japan's greater involvement with the world at large, makes it more difficult to accept unconditionally China's demands. When talking with officials one often hears some such remark as 'We are willing to negotiate with the Chinese, provided it is on the basis of equality' and they can point to Article (6) of the Chou-Tanaka communiqué as an indication that the Chinese have accepted this in principle.

Sovereignty in the East China Sea is another issue between the two states. It may be subdivided into the disputed ownership of the Senkaku (Tiaoyu) Islands and the disputes over the right to exploit the resources of the continental shelf. The claim to the Senkaku Islands has not been stressed recently in the Chinese press or official statements; however, although submerged, it remains and could easily surface again within the next few years to cause a crisis in Japan's relations with China. For this reason the problem merits some examination.

The Senkakus first came to public notice in 1968 when a geological survey under the auspices of the Economic Commission for Asia and the Far East reported the existence of rich oil deposits in the continental shelf between Japan and Taiwan. This was confirmed by a Japanese survey in the following years, which suggested that the area might become a particularly important source of oil for Japan. Until then, the Senkakus, a few uninhabited rocks with a combined area of 4·2 square miles, 118 miles northeast of Taiwan and about the same distance to the north of Ishigaki Island, which belongs to the Yaeyama group of islands of the Ryūkyū chain, had aroused no public interest whatsoever.

Once their importance was established, disputed claims were made to their ownership. The Japanese claimed possession through discovery. They also alleged that in 1881 the islands were marked on a map as forming part of the Ryūkyū chain and that they were formally designated as belonging to Ishigaki Island, being incorporated into that administrative entity. Until that date they had no juridical status. The islands were first 'occupied' three months before the signing of the Treaty of Shimonoseki in 1895, and, according to the Japanese, do not come under the same category as Taiwan and the Pescadores, which were ceded by China under the terms of that treaty.

The Japanese insist that there can be no question but that they belong to Japan. They were returned to Japan in 1972, with the Ryukyus, and form part of Okinawa Prefecture. Juridically, however, there is one fly in the ointment. The reference to Article (8) of the Potsdam Declaration in the Chou-Tanaka communiqué of 29 September 1972 implied Japanese admission of a territorial dispute because the Senkakus had never been specifically mentioned among the 'minor islands' or in the definition of the Ryukyus in the Treaty of San Francisco.[9]

The Chinese case rests on the claim that the islands were mentioned in documents of the Ming dynasty in the early sixteenth century. At that time they were linked to the Ryukyus whose Kings were paying tribute to the Chinese emperor. In the words of an article in *The People's Daily* of 29 December 1970, 'Like Taiwan, the Tiaoyu . . . Islands, etc., have been China's territories since ancient times. This is a historical fact no-one can change.'[10] Taipei and Peking are united in this respect. No official claim of sovereignty had been made by the government of the Republic of China at the time of the Japan-Republic of China Peace Treaty of 1952, but it tried to assert its claim once the islands had assumed an economic and strategic importance.

The whole issue is complicated by the ambiguous position of the United States and the problem of oil exploration in the East China Sea. When the question of ownership became a serious matter, the Department of State affirmed on 10 September 1970 that the Senkakus were part of the Ryukyus administered by the US, but that Japan enjoyed residual sovereignty over them and that they would be returned with the Ryukyus. As if to confirm this position, two firing ranges of the US Navy were reported to have been installed there. When the Reversion Agreement was being negotiated in 1971, the American position changed. Although it stood by the decision to return the islands, it adopted a studied neutrality over the disputed ownership and suggested that the matter be settled through negotiations between the interested parties or through third party mediation. The Reversion

Agreement was signed on 17 June 1971, a month before the announcement of President Nixon's visit to China.

The dispute over the Senkakus must of course be set in the context of claims to potential oil fields in the East China Sea. Japan, the Republic of Korea, and the government on Taiwan have demarcated large areas for exploration and eventual exploitation. Claims overlap and may become a fruitful source of future conflict among the three parties, to which one must add American companies. In 1970, for instance, the authorities in Taipei granted rights to American firms to explore resources around the Senkakus.[11]

All these arrangements left the People's Republic of China out of account. It has claimed rights over the continental shelf, which includes large tracts of the East China and South China seas. The military and naval operations against the South Vietnamese on the Paracel Islands in January 1974 have underlined the extent of these claims and the PRC's willingness to enforce them. On 15 August 1951, for instance, Chou En-lai had warned the negotiators of the Treaty of San Francisco that the Paracel Islands and Spratly Islands had always been Chinese territory.

The whole question is further complicated by the existence of differing principles of international law. A Convention in 1958 had laid down that national boundaries along a continental shelf should, in 'the absence of agreement, and unless another boundary line is justified by special circumstances, . . .' be defined by a median line between two states on opposite coasts or adjacent to each other. However, a decision of the International Court of Justice in 1969, with reference to the North Sea in Europe, had declared that a shelf is the natural prolongation of land and does not necessarily have to be divided up equally.

If the Convention were to apply, Japan could claim territorial rights to the west of the Okinawa Trench, a fissure which divides the continental shelf between the Ryūkyū chain and the Chinese mainland. Thus the Senkakus would fall under Japanese jurisdiction, although their proximity to Taiwan might raise further complications. If the ruling of the International Court were taken as the juridical basis, then Japanese territory might be limited to the shelf east of the Okinawa Trench and thus exclude the Senkakus.[12]

The dispute over the islands, like other issues over which Tokyo and Peking have differences, is brought forward or pushed into the background by the Chinese according to the dictates of strategy and the political climate. Thus, twelve months after the Satō-Nixon communiqué of November 1969, which inaugurated the negotiations for the return of Okinawa, the Chinese stridently asserted their rights over the Senkakus and denounced Japanese 'plots' to annex them. At the height of the *rapprochement* with Japan in 1972, Mr Chou was reported to have considered the Senkaku Islands a 'minor' matter.

The Japanese, too, have been flexible. Sometimes they have been firm in maintaining their position and have referred to the 'illegal' entry of Taiwanese ships into the territorial waters around the islands and the 'illegal' landing of crew members on them. The director of the 11th Regional Maritime Safety Headquarters at Naha once complained that 'Crew members of Taiwanese fishing vessels have no consciousness of guilt at all, and even if they are caught, they show a smiling face.'[13]

At other times the Japanese position has appeared to be more subtle and has suggested the familiar tactics of separating politics and economics. In January 1973, for instance, Mr Nakasone, then Minister of International Trade and Industry, had passed on to the Chinese a proposal for the joint exploration of the continental shelf. It is probable that he had in mind an arrangement similar to that concluded with the Republic of Korea on 30 January 1974 (but not ratified by Japan until the summer of 1977). Under that agreement, Japan and South Korea will jointly exploit the area south of Cheju Island while deferring a decision over the question of sovereignty. However, the Chinese were unwilling to consider such an arrangement. In March 1973 Nakasone stated that his ministry would not permit development until the controversy over sovereignty was settled.[14] Whether intentionally or not, he seemed to accept the existence of a dispute. This does not mean, of course, that Nakasone had any doubts about Japan's sovereign rights in the area.

In 1976 Japanese policy was caught on the horns of a dilemma over ratification of the agreement with South Korea for joint development of oil resources in the East China Sea. The Koreans ratified the agreement in July 1974 and steadily pressed the Japanese to do the same, but the latter were deterred by domestic opposition inspired by dislike of the South Korean régime and fear of Chinese and North Korean reactions. Japan sought China's prior understanding of the pact and would have preferred a multinational approach to the question of exploiting the resources of the East China Sea.[15] It did not receive satisfaction on the first count and is unlikely to succeed on the second unless it accepts the principle of Chinese sovereignty first.

The tangled issue of sovereign rights and claims in the seas between Japan, Korea, the Chinese mainland, and Taiwan was complicated further in the early months of 1977 by the problem of exclusive fishing zones, which has brought Japan into serious confrontation with the Soviet Union, for it bears directly on the Northern Territories issue, and a less acute dispute with the United States. Once again, Japan faces the task of reconciling important economic interests[16] with the need to accommodate two powerful and determined neighbours. In response to American and Russian actions, the Japanese government established a 200-mile national fishing zone around the coasts of the country but, significantly, will not enforce it in relation to South Korea or China unless they also establish such zones.

The decision taken on 26 January 1977 to extend Japan's territorial waters from three to twelve miles has raised new issues over the right of passage through the international waterways (the Straits of Tsugaru and Tsushima) which come under Japanese sovereignty. The problem here concerns Japan's policy of not permitting nuclear armed vessels to enter its territorial waters. Although the Chinese are not directly affected, they would undoubtedly welcome any measures which would restrict the freedom of Soviet nuclear submarines to pass through these waters into the Pacific Ocean.

All the outstanding political issues between the two countries have one thing in common. They cannot be dealt with in isolation but invariably involve Japan's policy towards other countries. This has, of course, been largely true ever since 1952, but until the 1970s there was only one third country which really mattered, the United States. Today the United States still retains great importance as a factor in Japan's China policy but it has ceased to be the filter through which that policy has to pass.

CHINA IN JAPAN'S RELATIONS WITH THIRD COUNTRIES

Three diagrams illustrate the changing international environment within which Japan has had to adjust its China policy during the post-war period.

Diagram I represents the situation during most of the first two decades after 1949. The relationship between the two groups of states was essentially hostile, although the degree of hostility fluctuated over time. Moreover, the picture becomes confused in the middle and late 1960s; first with the developing Sino-Soviet confrontation and then with China's withdrawal into isolation during the Cultural Revolution.

Diagram I

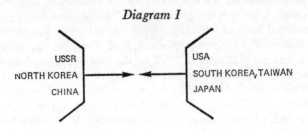

Diagram II

Diagram II reflects the state of affairs that emerged at the end of the 1960s and dominated the early 1970s. With the establishment of official relations between the United States and China, and between Japan and China, the reversion of Okinawa, the beginning of American disengagement from Indochina, and the increasing rivalry of China and the Soviet Union for the favours of other Asian countries, the confrontation between the two groups turned into two sets of triangular relationships. The connection between them was the close association between the United States and Japan, which remained at the centre of Japanese foreign policy. However, Japan was increasingly drawn into the sphere of Sino-Soviet rivalry and became the object of embarrassing attention from the two communist powers. The United States was simultaneously engaged in triangular diplomacy with the communist giants as Dr Kissinger tried to balance between détente with Russia and détente with China. His diplomacy was complicated by the different quality of each relationship. With Russia it was global and involved the central strategic balance; with China it was regional and involved the specific issues of Indochina and Taiwan. During this period there were some signs that the situation in Korea might move towards the kind of relationship which has come to exist between East and West Germany.

At the end of 1976 we seem to have a situation that is depicted in

Diagram III

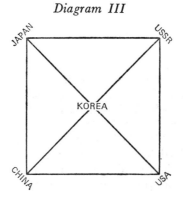

diagram III. The termination of the conflict in Indochina and the rapid withdrawal of the United States from the whole of Southeast Asia have opened a great debate over the American role in Northeast Asia. Both Japan and the Republic of Korea hope that the Americans will continue to guarantee their security. Neither can be certain of it. Instead of related triangular relationships, we have the four major powers occupying the corners of a field at whose centre lies Korea. The line linking the United States and Japan is essentially a co-operative one. The line linking the Soviet Union and China is essentially one of friction. The situation in Korea has deteriorated and is becoming more explosive, with evidence of increasing instability in the South.

Diagrams are useful as graphic presentations of relationships, but they obscure the untidiness of the real world. For instance, with the wisdom of hindsight we can now see that the Cold War was not a period of rigid confrontation between two clearly defined blocs. The changes in the Soviet Union after Stalin's death, the Sino-Soviet rift, the tensions within the Western Alliance which came to a head with de Gaulle's policies and the war in Vietnam, all presaged the trans-formation of the early 1970s. Yet, when the international situation in the Far East began to change rapidly with the inauguration of China's 'ping-pong diplomacy', Japan, in spite of an undercurrent drive for an independent China policy, was psychologically unprepared.

The Japanese were steeped in an 'anti-big power' ideology which they had acquired from the experience of the war and its aftermath. They had taken a wrong turning and they were not going to make the same mistake again. The military might of the United States and the USSR further discouraged any ideas of following that path once more. Moreover, Japan relied on the United States for its external security – without, however, a very clear perception of threat since the mid-1950s. In considering against whom and what Japan needed American protection, all seemed hypothetical and remote. To break through this fog would have meant raising specific questions about policies – a step which the government was not anxious to take, because of the possible impact of such questioning both on domestic politics and on Japan's external relations.

In the late 1970s Japan finds itself in a confusing international situation in which policy towards China cannot be separated from policy towards the Soviet Union, the United States, Korea, the whole Pacific-Asia region, and the Third World in general.

The impact of the Sino-Soviet conflict on Japan's China policy has already been described. The Japanese are attracted to the riches which Russia and China might be able to offer, but there is some reason for thinking that both prospects may be only mirages. This has already been proved true as far as the Tyumen oil field is concerned. The needs of both communist societies might become such that the margin to spare would not be worth a substantial Japanese investment. Moreover, Japan's capitalist enterprises would be severely restricted in socialist economies, which, from the point of view of the profitability of such vast undertakings, might present an unacceptable risk. One of the sticking points in negotiations with the Soviet Union is its demand for what the Japanese consider to be excessively low rates of interest. Finally, there is no evidence that imports of sources of energy and other raw materials from the USSR and China would meet more than a small fraction of Japan's overall requirements.

Added to these factors are other issues affecting Japan's diplomacy and security. A close alliance with either China or the Soviet Union is out of the question, for it would immediately alienate the other. It would impede independent action by Japan tailored to a rapidly changing world situation. Above all, it would destroy the alliance with the United States.

Japan's reluctance to move very close to one or other of the communist powers is due not only to fear of Chinese or Russian reactions, but also to the possible implications of such a move for relations with the United States. American involvement in Siberia would be welcome as a guarantee against sudden switches in Russian policy over supply and might also lessen the impact of Chinese hostility. Similarly, coordination with American policy over China would lessen any unwelcome attentions from the Soviet Union and would diminish the risk of an American-Chinese understanding which left out Japan.

It is, therefore, manifestly in Japan's interest to avoid an identification with either of its great neighbours on the Asian mainland and to keep the United States involved in the region – but in such a manner as to avoid provoking hostility from Russians and Chinese alike. Although the alliance with the United States remains the cornerstone of Japanese foreign policy, the events of 1972 mark a watershed in its significance for relations with China.

Suddenly, the alliance ceased to be a target of Chinese hostility. The Chinese leaders let it be known that they regard the Mutual Security Treaty as a welcome guarantee that Japan would not be tempted either to ally itself with Russia or to dream of military expansion. It is also seen as an obstacle to Russian expansion in the Pacific. The weight of Chinese propaganda is no longer thrown behind agitation against the treaty. This was noticeable during the generally ineffectual left-wing campaign in Japan against the terms of the reversion of the Ryūkyū Islands and in the continuing campaign against American bases in Japan.

The influence of Chinese attitudes on Japanese public opinion over issues related to the alliance with the United States has always been fairly marginal. Being able to point to Chinese reactions has, no doubt, helped sometimes to strengthen the argument against the security treaty. And among those with a particular ideological alignment, the Chinese line was obviously a major determinant in their position. Domestic politics and the dynamics of social psychology have, however, been the main influence on the attitudes of the public at large.

The change in Chinese attitudes is only one factor which has affected Japanese perspectives of the alliance. The succession of shocks administered by the American government since 1971 has had a more profound effect in forcing reassessment. The unheralded announcement of President Nixon's visit to China, the sudden imposition of import surcharges in August 1971, the pressures which forced the revaluation of the yen, the cut-off of soy-bean exports in 1973, all were seen by the Japanese as strong-arm tactics suited to naked power-politics rather than to the relationship of old and trusted associates. They have heightened awareness of the underlying conflict of interests between the two states, particularly in the economic field.

Moreover, the developing American-Soviet relationship, which has spread from efforts at joint management of the strategic balance and international crises to far-reaching commercial and technological relations, the frequent invocation of a new polycentric power structure, and the end of the war in Vietnam and the American withdrawal from Southeast Asia have strengthened the impression of a fundamental change in postwar American policy. The American approach to China, in particular, was seen as an exercise in 'jumping over Japan's head', which some Japanese attributed to dark Machiavellian designs.

Consideration of these matters has reinforced the doubts of all those who have had reservations about heavy dependence on the American alliance. They recall that, ever since the United States became involved in the east Asian region, its policies have been directed as much against as in support of Japanese interests. They reason that the postwar period might be only an interlude before the US returns to a more flexible policy in the region. At different times this could mean supporting China against Japan, or Japan against China, or both against the Soviet Union, or even joining with the Soviet Union against them. To support this argument one could point to two major reversals in postwar American policy. The first occurred in 1948, when the demilitarization and reform of Japan became secondary to building it up against communism. The second took place in 1971, with the approach to China.

Changing appreciations of the association with the United States have also been reflected in policy towards China. Consultations with the United States continue at all levels, but decisions are reached without necessarily making American reactions the major point of reference. The two countries have taken different stands over Taiwan. The independence of the Japanese approach towards China, which has always been there since 1952 – and even before – has now come into the open. In one respect, however, the Japanese government may have become more anxious than ever to stress the close association with the United States and that is in the field of security. When Americans were locked in confrontation with Russians and Chinese and when they enjoyed strategic superiority over both, the opposition could indulge in the luxury of attacking the Mutual Security Treaty and the government could afford to play down the security aspect of its responsibilities in the alliance. For, in so far as anything can be sure in international politics, the Americans could be counted upon to defend Japan against any attack from its powerful neighbours regardless of what the Japanese might think about the alliance. In the present situation Japan cannot be so sure about the American response, not least because one of the potential adversaries has increased its strategic power almost to the point of parity with the US.

In spite of a tendency in public statements to reduce the emphasis on the purely military aspects of the security treaty,[17] there has been a notable increase of Japanese concern with security since the summer of 1975. The establishment of a joint American-Japanese working group, to meet regularly to plan co-ordinated measures in defence of Japan,[18] has evoked only relatively mild opposition. Planning is against an eventual Soviet threat and one which might emerge as a result of events in Korea.

China does not pose a direct threat to Japan and would probably not be in a position to do so before the late 1980s. Although the security treaty has no immediate bearing on policy towards China, Japan regards the treaty as its contribution to ensuring the maintenance of American forces in Korea and the east Asian region. The tacit American guarantee of peace in the Strait of Taiwan, which emerged from the agreement between President Nixon and the Chinese leadership in February 1972, enables Japan to continue its search for improved relations with China while maintaining its interests in Taiwan without fear of the eruption of a major crisis in that area.

Korea is the touchstone of Japan's security policy. It poses two related questions. To what extent is Japan 'free' to intervene militarily in Korea if it feels threatened by developments in the peninsula? And to what extent would such an intervention involve the risk of direct confrontation with China?

After many years in which Korean affairs seemed more or less frozen, there are now signs of movement which may herald a dangerous phase in the international relations surrounding that particular area. These are developments from which Japan might find it difficult to remain aloof. Japan's relations with both Korean states are difficult. In fact, relations with the North can hardly be said to exist. There is a lobby, including members of the LDP, which agitates for the normalization of relations, and the slightest official gesture in the direction of Pyongyang arouses lengthy speculation about an imminent change in Japanese policy.[19] Relations with the South, on the other hand, are very close – some would say too close for comfort – and there has been a substantial economic penetration of the Republic of Korea. On the other hand, a series of incidents in recent years[20] has greatly embarrassed the Japanese government. Official policy towards the government in Seoul is generally inhibited by strong opposition to that régime in Japan.

The extent to which Japan would be 'free' to intervene in Korea is very largely a function of domestic politics. It would depend on the nature of the intervention and whether a perception of being threatened had created a strong enough national consensus to support whatever measures were taken. The risk of confrontation with China would depend on Chinese reactions to events in the peninsula.

So far we have considered areas in which China plays a part in Japanese policy, either because of geographical proximity or because of a substantial overlap of Chinese and Japanese interests in the area. Should China establish a strong influence in other parts of the world important to Japan it would also become a major consideration in the formulation of Japanese policy in those regions. So far the question has arisen only in one or two isolated instances and in the global context of the United Nations, where, long before the People's Republic occupied the Chinese seat, Japan began to press for a larger role for itself. It is perhaps too early at this writing to attempt an assessment of the impact of China on Japan's UN policy.[21] Chinese activities appear to have concentrated largely on countering Soviet influence in the Organization and have not been noticeable for any marked initiatives in furthering the work of the UN.

Very much the same pattern is seen in other fields. Chinese action seems designed to prevent the spread of Soviet influence and to offer an alternative socialist model. China's resources have been too slender to make a substantial impact through trade and aid, except in a few countries, such as Tanzania. One cannot, therefore, speak of serious economic competition between Japan and China in the Third World. This includes the Southeast Asian region, where the Japanese are not afraid of any Chinese penetration of their markets.[22] However, they are much more worried about safeguarding their sources of raw materials in the region. China's support of nationalist and revolutionary movements in Southeast Asia might interrupt supplies and could increase its potential leverage over Japan. Yet here, as elsewhere, China's principal objective is to counter the Soviet Union. This is particularly marked in its relations with the Indochinese states and the members of ASEAN. The Japanese thus find themselves in the cross-currents of the rival communist powers. They are interested in good relations with Vietnam (pro-Soviet) and with Cambodia (pro-China), so they are anxious to hear no evil, see no evil, and speak no evil.

CHINA IN DOMESTIC POLITICS

China continues to be an issue in domestic politics but in a new context. The debate no longer hinges on the problems of Taiwan versus the Mainland or over the existence of a two Chinas policy. This is not to say that the allegiance of the Japanese partisans has changed. The friends of the government on Taiwan and the friends of the government in Peking still face each other within the LDP, but over different issues. In 1975 and 1976 the debate has turned around the projected peace and friendship treaty, the weight to be given to Russian susceptibilities, and the position to be taken over American policy towards China.

Although the problem of relations with China has been exploited in the interests of the struggle for power within the Liberal-Democratic Party, it has always been of marginal importance in terms of the factional strife within the Party, mainly because adherents of Peking and Taipei were to be found within all the larger factions whose leaders found it politic to assume an equivocal position.

By 1976 China seemed to be further than ever from the preoccupations of the LDP leadership. It has been pointed out that there are three main schools of thought over China policy within the government party.[23] One consists of those who might be labelled 'pro-China', some, though not all, of whom are anti-Soviet. The second includes those who are hostile to Peking but who are not necessarily sympathetic to the Soviet Union. Instead, they tend to be pro-United States, pro-Taiwan, pro-Republic of Korea. The third school consists of those who are pro-Soviet, but, again, not necessarily anti-Chinese. Those elements in the Party that are more sympathetic to China are certainly in the ascendant over those favouring the Soviet Union.

It does not follow that those who dislike the Soviet Union want to see the government take an unequivocally pro-Chinese line. Rather, they fear that some official gestures like the foreign minister's 'tour of inspection' (from a safe distance) of the disputed Northern Territories and his remark that the Soviet Union was 'dangerous'[24] will exacerbate the Soviet Union and lead it to regard Japan as decidedly hostile. Hence, they have strong reservations about the inclusion of the anti-hegemony clause in the text of the treaty with China.

The changed perspective of the debate over China policy within the LDP is paralleled in the changed context of the opposition parties' view of China policy. Only within the JSP is there a clear schism between the pro-Chinese element, the great majority of the Party's Diet members, and the pro-Soviet element, increasingly strong among the party workers, under the influence of the Shakaishugi Kyōkai-ha.[25] The JCP looks on the French and Italian communist parties as its soul brethren and is almost equally alienated from the Soviet and Chinese parties. Kōmeitō and the Democratic-Socialist Party have in the past urged Japan to stay clear of the Sino-Soviet imbroglio.

Those in the opposition parties who incline towards China have also shifted their ground over the Mutual Security Treaty with the United States. The pro-Chinese group within the JSP includes some who want to revise the Party's hard-line anti-American policy and emphasize, instead, the need for a dialogue with the United States.[26] Kōmeitō, too, has modified its stand over the security treaty, and that modification has thrown some doubt over its position *vis-à-vis* China and the Soviet Union.[27]

It is true that there has been a slight indication of a change in the Russian perspective of the Japanese-American Alliance. It was much remarked that, in his address to the twenty-fifth Party Congress in February 1976, Mr Brezhnev omitted the customary attack on the security treaty as an obstacle to a peace treaty; modifications in the opposition parties' attitude to it might therefore be seen as a response to a modification in the Russian position. However, the very hard Soviet line over other issues in the bilateral relationship and the much more positive Chinese attitude to Japan's territorial claims, rearmament, and defence arrangements, indicate that the opposition parties, with their eyes on the electorate, are not likely to espouse a strong pro-Soviet line.

This view is reinforced by the fact that there are in the late 1970s no major tensions in Sino-Japanese relations, whereas the Northern Territories issue is a basic source of friction in relations with the Soviet Union and one on which there is near-unanimity among the Japanese.

The shifting of the ground over which policy towards China is debated within the LDP and the opposition parties and the indications that there is a slight tendency in official policy to lean towards China are reflected in the climate of public opinion. China has ceased to be an emotive issue for the public and the press. With Mao's death China's ideological appeal for students and some of the intelligentsia has also weakened.

There are no issues to excite feelings like those produced by the question of whether or not to establish relations with Peking. The projected treaty of peace and friendship is so much icing on the cake which had been baked in 1972. Since then, a number of administrative agreements have regulated the material relationship between the two countries. The treaty would, to change the metaphor, cross the 't's' and dot the 'i's' of a relationship firmly established. This is not to say that no new 'burning' issues may arise in the future – consideration of that problem is deferred to the next chapter – but merely to state the position at the beginning of 1977.

The events of the early 1970s lessened the perception of clear-cut issues in China policy. A distinction has to be drawn today between the existence of a generalized sentiment about China, which has some racial overtones, and a perception of international relations in which China may be regarded as one of a group of states with which Japan could be on more or less friendly terms.

Popular sentiment about China is not as strong in the late 1970s as it was in the 1950s, when it reflected a resurgent nationalism directed against American domination of Japan. The Japanese, preoccupied with the business of getting richer or, at least, staying rich, and enjoying all the benefits of a highly industrialized and technologically advanced society, are no longer very interested in China. The postwar generation has little direct knowledge or experience of China, and ignorance is reinforced by the lack of Chinese language teaching in schools and universities. In 1972 only 3 per cent of the language teachers in Japan's national universities taught Chinese, compared with 50 per cent who taught English and 35 per cent who taught German. Most of the rest taught either French or Russian.[28] Moreover, when taught at all, Chinese is treated as a dead language, much in the same way as Greek and Latin in Europe.

When Finance Minister Ōhira said of Mao Tse-tung (who had never been to Japan) that 'He had an oriental heart and as such knew Japan and its people',[29] he was indulging in the rhetoric that is popular among political leaders in Japan. Presumably he meant that Chinese and Japanese shared the heritage of the East Asian civilization, that their cultural and ethnic affinity enabled them to understand each other's thoughts and feelings at a level unattainable by Europeans and other outsiders.

Whether this is true or not, many Japanese appear to think that the Chinese share this view of the bilateral relationship, and that in itself is an important factor to be taken into account when discussing Japan's policy towards China. However, it does not follow that the concept of a 'special relationship' between the two peoples makes interstate relations any the smoother and easier. On the contrary, it may inject an element of stiff-necked moralism into negotiations, as over the projected treaty of peace and friendship, which renders a successful conclusion all the more difficult. The Japanese may be mistaken in interpreting the Chinese position thus, but their interpretation may influence their own negotiating position and complicate matters further.

NOTES

1 Ralph N. Clough, *East Asia and U.S. Security* (Washington, DC, The Brookings Institution, 1975), p. 109.
2 An example of the problems which can arise is found in Japan's periodic difficulties with Australia over the fulfilment of long-term agreements. For instance, in the early 1970s one of Australia's largest exporters of iron ore to Japan was forced to reduce its shipments by 6 per cent below the minimum level specified in a long-term contract with the Japanese steel industry (*The Financial Times*, 15 Mar 1972). On the other hand, Japanese interests have also suffered on occasion. Thus, the revalution of the Australian dollar led to a considerable increase in the price of wool and iron ore (*JTW*, 6 Jan, 12 May, and 2 June 1973). In 1976 Japan was in a difficult position because of its failure to meet prescribed quotas for sugar and beef imports. Over beef it eventually made considerable concessions to avoid Australian retaliation in other economic sectors of the bilateral relationship (*JTW*, 14 Feb 1976 and 29 Jan 1977).
3 *The Petroleum Economist*, vol. XLII, no. 3, Mar 1975, pp. 96–7; vol. XLII, no. 5, May 1975, p. 166; *JTW*, 28 Dec 1974, 13 Mar and 3 Apr 1976, 9 Apr 1977.
4 A Chinese barrel of fairly good quality (low sulphur but high wax content) oil cost $13.50, while a barrel of comparable quality from Indonesia was priced at $12.60. *JTW*, 28 Dec 1974.
5 At a time when the Japanese were seriously interested in the development of the Tyumen oil field, the Russians rather suddenly suggested a cut in the amount of oil to be supplied annually to Japan, from a range of 25–40 million tons originally planned to 25 million tons as the maximum. One of the reasons for the switch may have been a desire to strengthen their bargaining position in negotiations for a bank loan. From the Japanese point of view, the reduction of supplies would have made the return on investment much less profitable. *JTW*, 15 Sep 1973.
6 *JT*, 24 Jan 1976.
7 *The International Herald Tribune*, 21 July 1976; *The Financial Times*, 23 July 1976; *JTW*, 24 and 31 July 1976.
8 *JTW*, 31 July 1976.
9 Denise Folliot, ed., *Documents on International Affairs 1951* (London, OUP for RIIA, 1954), p. 613.
10 *Survey of China Mainland Press*, no. 4813, pp. 134–6.
11 John K. Emmerson, *Arms, Yen & Power: the Japanese Dilemma* (New York, Dunellen, 1971), p. 192. There is a good map in *Strategic Survey*

1970 (London, Institute for Strategic Studies, 1971), p. 71, which shows the overlapping claims of Japan, South Korea, and Taiwan in the East China Sea.

12 Conference on the Law of the Sea, 23–9 Apr 1958, d) Convention on the Continental Shelf, Article 6, Doc. A/Conf. 13/L.55, reproduced in Gillian King, ed., *Documents on International Affairs 1958* (London, OUP for RIIA, 1962), p. 563; International Court of Justice, *Reports of Judgments, Advisory Opinions and Orders 1969: North Sea Continental Shelf Cases, Judgment of 20 February 1969* (Leyden, Sijthoff), pp. 53–4.

13 *Tokyo Shimbun*, 8 Dec 1972.

14 *JTW*, 17 Mar 1973.

15 China had declared the Japan-South Korea Agreement to be null and void because it infringed China's sovereign rights (*JTW*, 22 Mar 1975). The deputy director of the Asian Affairs Bureau in the Gaimushō told the House of Representatives Foreign Affairs Committee that Japan wanted *all* (my italic) parties to come together to discuss exploitation of the East China Sea, although he did not see much hope of that in the near future. 'In this perspective, the Government signed the treaty with South Korea.' (*JTW*, 15 May 1976.)

16 Japan is the world's biggest fishing nation and it is estimated that more than 40 per cent of its annual catch has been taken from other countries' 200-mile fishery zones.

17 Administrative policy speech by Prime Minister Miki Takeo at the seventy-fifth session of the National Diet, 24 Jan 1975 (text of speech supplied by Ministry of Foreign Affairs, Tokyo).

18 The new organ was set up as a result of the talks between the Director-General of the Defence Agency, Sakata Michita, and US Secretary of Defense Schlesinger, held in late Aug 1975 in Tokyo (*JTW*, 6 Sep 1975). A year later, the press devoted a great deal of attention to Soviet naval and air activities around Japan. There is a detailed account of these activities, plus a 'log' of events and accompanying map for the period between May and July 1976, in *JTW*, 28 Aug 1976.

19 One such occasion was the meeting between Japan's chief delegate, and former Foreign Minister, Kimura Toshio and the chief North Korean delegate during the UNCTAD Conference in Nairobi, in May 1976. They met at a reception given by Kimura – this was the first encounter of senior government representatives from the two countries at an official function. *JTW*, 22 May 1976.

20 The incidents have included the kidnapping of the South Korean opposition leader, Kim Dae-jung, from a hotel room in Tokyo in Aug 1973, the attempted assassination of President Park in Aug 1974 by a Korean resident in Japan, and the sack of the Japanese Embassy in Seoul in Sep 1974, following a statement from a senior official in the Gaimushō that Japan did not regard the South Korean government as the only legitimate government in the whole Korean peninsula.

21 It is perhaps noteworthy that the two countries have taken opposing positions on a number of international issues. They include the law of the

sea and the control of nuclear arms. At the UNCTAD meeting in 1972 and the Stockholm Conference on the Environment in the same year, they were also on opposing sides. Clough, p. 79.

22　This has not always been so. An element of friction entered into economic relations in the late 1950s though too much can be made of this as it did not become a permanent issue between the two countries. Chinese exports to the Southeast Asian region began to compete with similar goods from Japan and caused setbacks to Japanese sales. In 1957 the Foreign Ministry accused China of infiltrating the regional market at Japan's expense by exploiting the overseas Chinese community, by price manipulation, and through loans from the Central Bank of China – ignoring the fact that Japan was also infiltrating the regional market under the guise of reparations. A government survey published in July 1958 purported to show that Chinese exports of manufactured goods posed a serious threat to Japan's trade in the area. The products included textiles, cement, and cheap iron manufactures. Leng, pp. 67–8.

23　Sase Masamori. 'Japan zwischen China und der Sowjetunion', *Europa Archiv*, no. 15, 10 Aug 1976, pp. 510–11.

24　Ibid., p. 514.

25　Ibid., pp. 510–11.

26　Ibid. See also *JTW*, 27 Sep 1975 and 3 Jan 1976.

27　Sase, pp. 510–11; *JTW*, 17 Jan and 7 Feb 1976.

28　Maeda Yōichi, *JTW*, 9 Sep 1972.

29　In a tribute to Mao on his death, as reported in the *JTW*, 18 Sep 1976.

5 The Outlook for Japan's Relations with China

As he tries to peer into the future the author is caught between the wish to present a clearly sketched, cogently argued scenario, and the need to handle complex material full of variables and qualified by many 'ifs' and 'buts'.

In thinking about the future course of Japanese policy towards China we have the advantage of starting with a number of models put forward and discussed by other authors. One model envisages a collision course between the two countries in which conflicting interests lead to confrontation.[1] Another is based on the opposite assumption : a gradual drawing together of Japan and China as a result of common interests and their 'natural' affinity, perhaps leading to a kind of osmosis.[2] A third model envisages a China which is seen by the Japanese as having only a marginal importance in the pattern of their overall interests, which are predominantly economic and global.[3]

Each model has the virtues of clarity and consistency but some of the assumptions on which each is based may easily turn out to be false. Thus, the first model is built on the assumption of an irreconcilable conflict of interests in Southeast Asia, or the existence of a basic adversary relationship which may eventually be exacerbated by an arms race between the two countries. The second model presupposes that their complementary economies and a common cultural and ethnic background will draw Japanese and Chinese together against the 'outsiders'. The third takes Japan's continued economic growth and expansion as axiomatic and assumes a widening gap between the development of Japan and China.

None of these assumptions is unreasonable if we take the present as our point of departure. But suppose Southeast Asia declines as an area of economic or strategic interest to Japan, or that, because of a common concern about the Soviet Union or some other threat, the Japanese and Chinese fail to see each other as rivals? A similar transformation has happened to the French and West Germans, though thirty years ago few Frenchmen were prepared to stop worrying about a potential German threat. Suppose, also, that Japan continues its present military policy more or less unchanged?

The osmosis thesis depends on the Japanese and Chinese becoming more and more interested in each other, but in fact the range of direct contact between the two countries in the past thirty years has been rather limited and there are few signs of a change in the pattern. On the other hand, the picture of a Japan whose interests led it to turn its back on east Asia is based on the assumptions that Japan will continue to have free access to markets the world over, which will absorb its exports and investments, and that China will not be a great economic power by the end of the century.

The pitfalls of attempting to predict the future are obvious. However, it is also the case that predictions forcefully presented and widely held may, for those very reasons, become self-fulfilling. Those responsible for making policy may come to believe that what has been predicted will really happen, and they will take specific measures and make plans accordingly. This, in turn, may elicit the 'appropriate' response from the other side, with the result that the two parties interact in what they have come to believe is an inevitable trend in their relationship. The patterns of alliances and crises before the First World War might be considered an example of such interaction. The pattern of the strategic nuclear arms race between the two superpowers is another.

Models of the future are undoubtedly useful in providing a conceptual framework for discussion or policy-making; I have mentioned their dangers in order to warn the reader not to expect a clear and sharply drawn picture of Japan's future China policy by the time he has reached the end of this chapter. I shall, however, attempt to make some estimate of the future impact and importance of specific issues in Japan's relations with China and then discuss the three determinants which, I think, will govern the course of Japanese policy: developments in Japan, developments in China, and the evolution of the international environment. The discussion has been limited generally to the outlook for the 1980s.

THE FUTURE IMPORTANCE OF SPECIFIC ISSUES

The Economic Interest
The conundrum here is to answer the following questions. How keen will Japan be to trade with China and to tap its resources? And how necessary will Japanese goods, technology, and capital be for China's economic development?

On paper, at least, the potential for a close economic partnership seems obvious, and such a link – between China's enormous reservoir of manpower and vast untapped natural resources and Japan's highly developed industries and financial, technical, and managerial resources – would be formidable indeed. One can think of many benefits and attractions in an expanded economic association with China, but they must be set against the constraints that arise in this particular bilateral relationship and the limitations it might impose on Japan's global interests. The vision of economic complementarity between the two countries recalls the Japanese dream about China in the 1920s and 1930s, but the drive behind it may not be so strong.

The constraints include all the uncertainties about China's economy and policies, and China's unwillingness to become heavily dependent on any foreign power, let alone Japan, for its economic development. They also include the limitations of China as a trading partner and the likely direction of Japan's economic development.

Apart from natural resources, what has China to offer Japan? Moreover, the limits of the trade in primary materials have already been indicated by the declining expectations of the amount of oil Japan may buy from China and by the growing pressure from the agricultural lobby within Japan against agricultural products from China, which are among the most important items in its exports to Japan. There is also a continuing interest in developing economic relations with the Soviet Union. Japan's resources could not meet both Russian and Chinese requirements in capital and equipment for large-scale development of their natural resources.

The foregoing remarks assume that Japan will continue to be one of the world's giant importers of industrial raw materials and mineral fuels, as well as a giant exporter of heavy manufactures (machinery, metals, motor vehicles, ships, etc.). However, if Japan's economy follows the widely predicted course of moving away from dependence on heavy industry, one may expect a rapid increase in the present trend to invest in manufacturing industry abroad and, at home, an accelerated development of industries depending on very advanced technology but requiring less energy and raw materials. In addition, Japan might eventually assume the role that Britain played in the nineteenth century and become the world's economic middleman through its services as a banker, investor, insurer, and carrier.[4] Even if one does not accept some of the more fanciful visions of Japan's economic future – and there are some experts who counter them by postulating a structural readjustment of the economy in which social welfare goals will take precedence and the GNP growth rate will decline[5] – all indications point to the conclusion that while China may acquire a gradually increasing share of Japan's foreign trade, it is likely to be very much smaller than the pre-war share – that is, provided there is no major upheaval to break the likely patterns of Japan's economic development.

Such an upheaval would probably take place as a result of a dramatic change in the international economic environment which might drive the Japanese into seeking a close Sino-Japanese partnership. One can imagine the Japanese being shut out of the European and North American markets after a bitter trade war, or, for economic and political reasons, being deprived of important sources of oil and raw materials. In those circumstances the lure of China might become very compelling indeed. The turbulence of the international economic and monetary systems in recent years certainly does not rule out such developments. However, even if they were to come about and regardless of the form they took, Japan could not, as it did in the past, fall upon China as an area for domination. It can no longer impose its will on the Chinese. Instead of using force to achieve its ends it would have to resort to persuasion and be prepared to make substantial concessions.

The Political and Security Interest

There is no denying that combustible material is lying about which might become the cause of a sharp deterioration in Japan's relations with China. The disputed claims over the Senkakus and over economic rights in the East China Sea presently lie dormant. But so for twenty years was the Chinese claim to the Paracel Islands and then suddenly the Chinese seized the islands with a short, sharp, armed strike. Thus, the question remains whether the dormant territorial disputes between China and Japan might not prove to be a time-bomb.

That possibility must not be ruled out. One can imagine a variety of incidents which might set it off. How would the Japanese react, for example, to a Chinese seizure of a survey vessel off the Senkakus?[6] The Japanese response would no doubt be influenced by the state of China's nuclear capability. Whatever the outcome of such a crisis, the initiative for provoking it would rest with China. The Japanese, after all, are in possession of the Senkaku Islands and have reached some measure of agreement with other interested parties for the exploration and exploitation of zones of the continental shelf. In attempting to assess the potential danger in the situation, it is necessary to weigh up various considerations which would affect Chinese policy.

Assuming that there are very substantial riches under the continental shelf, how important are they to the Chinese economy? One could answer this by pointing to the undoubted resources in China itself and in the immediate coastal waters. For some time these should be more than adequate to meet the requirements of the national economy and the Chinese would probably need foreign technology and capital to develop them. Thus, it becomes a question of whether they would be willing to see the continental shelf exploited by the Japanese and others in return for some arrangement involving the transfer of technology, the payment of royalties, and the recognition of China's legal rights. Would the Chinese, as has been their tradition, be satisfied with an agreement over principle while allowing the Japanese to gain material benefit? Behind such considerations lies the fundamental question of the importance to China of good and friendly relations with Japan.

The existence of disputed claims is an uncomfortable reminder that there is a serious potential for conflict between the two countries. Although these claims seem unlikely to be a prime source of hostility they could become a major issue if there is a sharp deterioration in the international relations of the region, or if either China or Japan assumes a rigid and aggressive posture as a result of domestic political and economic pressures.

Events in Taiwan might be another cause of conflict. In spite of Japan's recognition that the future of Taiwan has to be decided by the Chinese and the fact that China has not made Taiwan a major issue in the negotiations for a peace and friendship treaty, a serious crisis between Taipei and Peking might encourage right-wing elements in Japan to support Taiwanese independence. This could have the effect of drawing a Japanese government, whether willingly or not, into a conflict with China.

In the event of such a development, Japan would not be restrained by inhibitions arising out of the aftermath of World War II. The Japanese tend to regard Taiwan as having a different relationship to their country from that of Korea, Manchuria, and other lands conquered in the past. That attitude is reinforced by reports of pro-Japanese sentiments among the Taiwanese, although the Kuomintang government and those Chinese who came to the island with Chiang Kai-shek's armies in 1949 do not share them. The Japanese also have a bad conscience over the 'betrayal' of the Nationalist Republic of China in 1972. This is an important factor in a society where feelings of honour and shame play a significant part in social attitudes. An influential section of the LDP has never been reconciled to the 'abandonment' of Taiwan implicit in official policy since 1972.

More material factors may also have their part in Japan's interest in Taiwan. It is the repository of large investments and it occupies a strategic position on the routes to the south and southwest. Furthermore, many Japanese, particularly among the ruling élites and in business circles, are fearful of and hostile to the spread of communism. Hence, in a confrontation between the Mainland and Taiwan they might look upon the latter as a bulwark in the defence of the 'true culture' of the East.

It is important to note, however, that the bias of some business circles does not necessarily coincide with any tendencies to back an independent Taiwan. Many businessmen would not support such a policy. They tend to favour an understanding with Peking which accepts the authority of the People's Republic over the island while the Japanese would retain a modified version of their investment stake combined with a preferential export position. This policy is based on the assumption that Taiwan will become part of Communist China within the next five or, at most, ten years. In pursuit of this approach, there is some evidence of an informal sounding-out of the government in Peking by Japanese firms before decisions are taken with regard to new investments or loans.

In sum, Japanese policy towards Taiwan will be determined by the importance attached to the material stake in Taiwan's economy, by considerations of national security, particularly as they affect the sea routes which pass by the island, and by the interplay of domestic politics and national emotions. However, the trigger of any dramatic change in policy lies in Taiwan itself.

In the past thirty years there has been little evidence that the Taiwanese independence movement has made substantial headway. Nor has there been much sign of a merger between the postwar Chinese settlers and the Taiwanese population. Yet, the country is now economically and socially so developed as to have some claim to be considered an independent entity in the world. This claim becomes stronger with every year that passes. Chiang Kai-shek is dead. The remaining Kuomintang leaders are ageing. Within a few years those born on the island, whether of native Taiwanese or immigrant parents, will move into positions of responsibility. They do not know the Mainland and have little reason to feel that they belong to it.

There are at least three alternative prospects for the island's future. There could be a gradual reunification with the Mainland; Taiwan could renounce its claim to be the Republic of China and issue a formal declaration of independence as the Republic of Taiwan; it could become the centre of a military conflict with the Mainland, which might involve other powers.

Much would depend, of course, on the policy of Communist China. How important is Taiwan to China? Is it mainly a symbol of Chinese unity and would the Chinese, once the principle of Taiwan's subordination to the mainland government was formally accepted by the islanders, allow them to develop socially and economically without necessarily adopting the system of the Mainland?

It is possible that the rival groups of a severe power struggle in Peking will bid for Taiwanese support by making promises about the island's future. Alternatively, it is possible that a power struggle in Taiwan may lead rival factions to appeal to the mainland Chinese and the Americans, or Japanese, for support. Whatever the course of events, it is most likely that Japan would, in the light of its widespread interests, seek to adjust to changes in Taiwan and its status rather than take an active part in determining its future.

A Chinese absorption of Taiwan that left Japan free to pursue its special economic interests on the island would be the most acceptable solution. A formal declaration of independence would have no adverse effects on economic relations, and might possibly even further them, but it would be wholly unacceptable to Peking and would create very dangerous tensions in the area. In such a situation the government on the Mainland might call on Japan to impose an embargo on all dealings with the island. Japan would demur but it would be forced to choose between the Mainland and Taiwan, and there can be little doubt that it would choose the former.

Any outbreak of violence is bound to be very embarrassing to the Japanese, particularly if it led to the use of American bases in Japan for support operations. Although the Japanese would seek to avoid direct involvement, a crisis in the Taiwan area might quickly become an explosive issue in domestic politics.

A third potential crisis area is Korea. Japanese security may be seen as directly affected by events in the peninsula. A revolutionary situation might develop in the South, result in the overthrow of the present régime and lead to unpredictable reactions from the North. A period of disorder and civil war in the South would threaten Japan's economic interests. The possibility that the whole peninsula might pass under the control of the communist régime in the North would be very alarming. The possibility that one or other of the communist giants might intervene and establish an ascendancy over both halves of the country would be even more alarming and could provoke a Japanese reaction that would completely change postwar defence policy. Moreover, despite restraints on the dispatch of Japanese forces overseas, scattered evidence suggests that the Japanese authorities are inclined to regard South Korea as within their defence perimeter.[7]

A direct confrontation between China and Japan over Korea seems remote. It is unlikely because the Chinese could not be sure of Russian and American reactions to their intervention in the peninsula and because the Japanese could not face China, let alone China and the Soviet Union, without active American support. However much Japan might be tempted to intervene to protect its interests, the tightly enmeshed four-power relationships over Korea should inhibit it from doing so.

It is a fair assumption that most Japanese see the national interest served best by a continuation of the restraint which in the past the Soviet Union and China have imposed on the North Koreans and the United States has imposed on the South Koreans. That is why President

Carter's policy of withdrawing ground forces from South Korea has provoked a very nervous reaction in Japan, because it has raised a host of unwelcome questions. What will be the effect on the government of President Park? Will it become less amenable to the restraining influence of the United States? What will be the reactions of the communists in the North? Can the United States retain the same credibility of its security guarantee to the South without American divisions on the ground? Most serious of all, from the Japanese point of view, will increasing American reliance on bases in Japan, to make the guarantee to South Korea effective, reduce Japan's freedom of manœuvre during a crisis in the peninsula by automatically tying Japan to American policy? A nagging feeling lurks behind these questions that, despite official statements to the contrary in Washington, the American troop withdrawal from Korea will not stop at that level but might be a prelude to further disengagement from South Korea and eventually from Japan.

Abdication of all American responsibility for the security of South Korea might have one of several consequences: a swift assault from the North on a demoralized enemy; the collapse of the régime in the South; an attack by the government in Seoul against the North, in the knowledge that time was not on its side. The government of the South might also make a determined attempt to acquire nuclear weapons. There are plans for a civil nuclear programme based on imported technology. The country also deploys aircraft capable of carrying nuclear weapons. However, it has been estimated that approximately ten years would pass between a decision to make nuclear explosives and the first explosion. There are in fact many restraints which would make a nuclear-armed South Korea unlikely.[8]

The contingency is worth mentioning only because such a development would be the most likely reason for Japan to acquire nuclear weapons. It would be seen as a challenge from an unstable neighbour of inferior status—which might create a mood of public support for such a fundamental reversal of national policy. Moreover, complete abandonment of South Korea by the United States would bring into question the whole structure of the American-Japanese security system.

There is good reason to think that the Chinese, too, are not altogether happy at the prospect of an American withdrawal from South Korea. North Korean President Kim Il-sŏng is nobody's stooge, but the Chinese are wary lest a crisis in the Korean peninsula provide the Soviet Union with an opportunity to exercise a decisive influence on the course of events. Chinese policy towards Korea is reactive and will be guided by assessments of the danger that any of the other major powers, principally of course the Soviet Union, will acquire a hegemonic position over the peninsula.

In the long run, the strength of Korean nationalism will prove to be the best barrier to foreign domination. However, in the face of continuing hostility between the two Korean régimes and from the perspective of the delicate structure of international relations in the region, conflict might be avoided if the three neighbouring powers and the United States could work out a substantial agreement providing for their effective opposition to an attack from either half of Korea on the other, as well as for their own non-involvement in the internal affairs of the two Korean states. That would be in the best interests of Japan and China.

Over Korea, as over Taiwan and the territorial issues, Japan will react to changes in the existing situation rather than initiate them. The dominant feature in all the areas I have considered is Japan's uncertainty about China's intentions. This will encourage the Japanese government to follow a policy of insurance, which might present it with at least four options : a continued reliance on the security arrangements with the United States; attempting to foster an interlocking series of agreements between the four major powers in northeast Asia (the Soviet Union, the United States, China, and Japan); a policy of strict neutrality; endeavouring to draw closer to China. Each one of these choices would present problems and difficulties.

While continued adherence to the American alliance would be an eminently sensible choice for a Japanese government in an uncertain and fluid international climate, it may well pursue this line of policy with diminishing conviction. Lack of confidence in the durability of the partnership stems from the changing strategic environment and from Japanese perceptions of American policy.

The problem of security is summed up in the debate over the reliability of the American deterrent. A few years ago the debate focused on the danger that Japan might be drawn into America's Asian wars. Today, the problem is different. The question is for how much longer Japan can rely on the credibility of the American commitment. Even if Japan met the much repeated American request for greater participation in the security arrangements of the region, the American strategic deterrent may lose its effectiveness and leave Japan exposed to the pressures of its giant neighbours.

Although China's nuclear capability is far behind that of either the United States or the Soviet Union, the Chinese have several options open to them in the development of their nuclear forces. Some might pose a greater potential threat to Japan than others. The extent to which the United States would be prepared to counter such a threat would depend on the degree to which its own territory and forces were threatened and on calculations of the effect of Chinese power on the nuclear balance with the Soviet Union. This kind of analysis is not only contingent on the military factor but on the state of the political relationship between the three powers.[9]

We may hear more in Japan of the kind of debate over the credibility of the American deterrent that took place in Europe in the late 1950s and in the 1960s. The issues and context are of course different. The development of Japan's industrial nuclear programme has created opportunities for a decision in favour of a weapons programme during a period of international tension. There remain very considerable political, psychological, and technical obstacles in the way of creating a Japanese nuclear deterrent, but decisions are not always based on a detached and judicious consideration of the issues involved.

Should there be great doubt about the reliability of the American guarantee against a potential threat from the Soviet Union, a Japanese government might turn to the second option and try to promote an international security system in the region.

The Soviet Union pushed the idea of an Asian collective security system for some years. Lately it appears to have been superseded by proposals for a series of bilateral agreements which, collectively, would ensure the *status quo* in Asia. It would be difficult for Japan to enter into either a multilateral or a bilateral agreement in the face of open Chinese hostility. The second option would, therefore, be acceptable only if there was a substantial lessening of tension between the Soviet Union and China. Even if the Russians tried to tempt Japan with some concessions over the Northern Territories in return for entering into a bilateral agreement, it is unlikely that Japan would entertain such a *quid pro quo* if it meant a serious deterioration in relations with China.

The third option of strict neutrality is attractive. The chief objection to it would come from within the country. There would be strong opposition from certain political and industrial circles, on the grounds that the great benefits which Japan had gained in recent decades stemmed from its ability to pursue its policies under American protection, other states being well aware that any threats to its national interest might well provoke US involvement. Hence, neutrality would require very substantial rearmament, which might please some politicians and industrialists but would impose a strain on the economy, arouse the bitter opposition of all those who support the spirit of Article 9 (the celebrated war-renouncing clause) of the Constitution, and have the effect of frightening Japan's neighbours. The alternative of *unarmed* neutrality, which has been the policy of the JSP for many years, would be opposed on the grounds that it would leave Japan defenceless against pressures from its neighbours. In spite of the Constitution and the postwar pacifism of the Japanese people, recent opinion polls indicate that a substantial majority of the people accept the need for the Self-Defence Forces.

The last option of trying to draw closer to China would be open to the same hesitations as any attempt to secure bilateral or multilateral agreements involving the Soviet Union. Only in this case the hostility and unpredictable consequences would come from the Russian side.

It is very likely that, given the continuation of the present international situation in the region, and that is a big assumption, Japanese policy will incline towards maintaining the security agreement with the United States and securing some kind of a code of international behaviour in the region through agreements with all the major powers there. Such a policy might offer the best chance of keeping Japan out of armed conflicts.

Ideology and Status
Speculation about the impact of political and social change in Japan on policy towards China may be appropriate when we discuss one of the three determinants which will shape the relationship with China. The problem here is to assess whether cultural and ideological factors may become important in shaping policy.

The assessment of these factors is very difficult. The subject matter is somewhat insubstantial and discussion of it tends to be based on impressions rather than 'hard' facts. To be sure, a good deal of material has been accumulated and analysed by psephologists, public opinion researchers, and social psychologists,[10] but their findings are necessarily tentative and often contradictory. Moreover, traditional philosophies and perceptions of the world, which arose out of the east Asian physical, social, and cultural environment, have been modified so much since the Second World War that they are at best imperfect guides to Japanese behaviour.

For these reasons, it is tempting to overlook or doubt the significance of values and perceptions which arise from the cultural and historical background of a country. Some evidence does, however, exist, which points to the significance of these factors in Japanese relations with China since 1945.[11] They include perceptions of the international order, concern over image, over status, and a feeling of kinship which may enter into relations with China and other east Asian nations but not into relations with other countries.

Before east Asia was absorbed into the world system imposed by Western dominance, relations within the region were governed by a concept which was different from that of the balance of power. Without entering into a long discussion here,[12] the East Asian concept, which had its roots in the central position of China and the develop-

E

ment of Chinese thought, revolved around the idea of hegemony, which was a concept of hierarchy based more on moral superiority than on physical domination. The breakdown of hegemony was regarded as a disturbance of the natural order of things. Since China occupied such a central position, both culturally and geographically, it followed that the power which was installed there would exercise hegemony over the region. Such a view explains to some extent the Japanese concern over the control of China in the last century.

The postwar era has witnessed a major change in both Chinese and Japanese perceptions of the international order. The most striking evidence of this is their opposition to the hegemony of any one power in the region. Certainly, this opposition arises from their sense of inferiority *vis-à-vis* the Soviet Union and the United States rather than from the deliberate shedding of a philosophy of international relations. None the less, the fact that both countries have publicly renounced any ambition to seek hegemony is an important break with traditional thinking. And yet, the negotiations over this issue and other issues since the war betray a Japanese suspicion that the Chinese are seeking acceptance of their moral hegemony, as in the Chinese insistence on prior agreement over the basic principles, as formulated by China, which should govern the relations between the two states.

Japanese sensitivity may also be observed in the concern about prestige and status, in reactions to China's ideological appeal, and in reactions to Chinese moralism. As China becomes more involved in the affairs of the United Nations and seeks to play a more active part in world politics, Japan is likely to stress its own importance in international affairs and wish to be seen as playing a significant part in them. The recently renewed Japanese claim to a permanent seat on the Security Council of the UN illustrates this tendency.

As for China's ideological appeal, apart from the most dedicated Maoists, the great majority of Japanese do not think that China offers a suitable model for Japan. This feeling is likely to continue and is strengthened by the rather superior airs which the Japanese allow themselves when it comes to economic development. There is little reason to believe that China's popularity rating will jump dramatically and replace the predilections of the Japanese public for some Western countries.

However, there is one sense in which China has exercised an ideological attraction over the Japanese and may continue to do so. We have noted how relations with China have played their part in postwar politics as a weapon with which to belabour opponents and as a symbol of the search for national identity. The ideology of the 'new China' is a symbol of that country's rebirth. The Japanese are still looking for something to mark their rebirth after the collapse of 1945.

They thought they had found it in their 'economic miracle'. But in the 1970s they are not quite so sure. In time of crisis, and assuming that China is not in disarray, China may exercise a certain appeal. It will be the 'nationalist' component of Chinese marxism which may be so appealing, not the marxist ideology in itself. The collectivist aspect of Chinese society is not likely to hold such terrors for the Japanese as it may have for people in Western countries, steeped in a tradition of individualism.

The moralistic tone of Chinese propaganda and official pronouncements would, on the other hand, arouse resentment. We have noted that the Japanese Communist Party resented the moralistic tone of their Chinese comrades. There is no reason to think that the Japanese, whether communist or not, will be any the more inclined to accept moral lectures in the future. The Japanese perception, whether right or wrong, that the Chinese will take a hard and severe line in negotiations because of the bonds of kinship between the two peoples, will ensure that the Japanese response to Chinese overtures will be cautious and circumspect. The sensitivity of public opinion to the cultural and ideological issues will, therefore, have some bearing on the course of Japan's policy.

The issues discussed so far, whether taken in isolation or together, are not likely to result in a Japanese policy of either close friendship or open hostility towards China. Their significance will be decided within the general context of relations with China, largely shaped by the three determinants mentioned at the beginning of this chapter.

THE DETERMINANTS OF JAPANESE POLICY

Developments within Japan
Let us assume that Japan will enjoy continued economic growth, probably at a lower rate than obtained in the 1960s and early 1970s, and that this implies a continued rise in the standard of living of the average Japanese, as well as increasing economic interests overseas through trade, investment, and services. In that case it is reasonable to suppose that Japan will continue to enjoy a basic social stability. However, the stability of the political scene is a different matter.

By the end of 1974 the LDP was in serious disarray. Its traditional policy of economic growth seemed to be in ruins. It was discredited by scandal and torn by fierce factional strife. Its domination of the Diet was threatened for the first time since the Party was founded. By the end of 1976 the Lockheed scandal had all but torn the Party apart and it retained control of the Lower House of the Diet by a whisker. Yet the closer the opposition parties seem to power, the fiercer their own dissensions and the more incredible their claim to be an effective alternative.

Whether the LDP survives and recovers or breaks up into rival conservative parties, or whether there will be a new constellation of political forces leading to a reformist government, such shifts in power would not necessarily mean major changes in perceptions of Japan's interests and in the policies necessary to sustain them. A government dominated by moderate left-wing parties might take a more detached view of the United States and move Japan towards non-alignment. On the other hand, the recent change of nuance by some of the opposition parties towards the Mutual Security Treaty does not suggest a sudden and dramatic shift away from the United States.

Suppose, however, that the social equilibrium in Japan is upset by economic difficulties or some other upheaval, and that this resulted in revolutionary pressures, then one might have to contemplate a different scenario. One could envisage the emergence of a strong socialist/communist régime, or, equally well, a reaction from the extreme right against the government's socialist measures, which might create a national mood in favour of right-wing authoritarianism. Again, however, left or right authoritarian governments in Japan do not imply dramatic and far-reaching changes in foreign policy.

A leftist government would certainly loosen the connection with the United States, but that need not mean an alliance with either China or the Soviet Union. The world is becoming used to the emergence of communist or socialist governments, or parties, that pursue radical policies at home but have views on national interests and international relations which are barely distinguishable from the views of liberal or right-wing authoritarian governments. The same, or similar, difficulties in dealing with economic, territorial, political, and psychological issues in the relationship with China would face a left-wing government in Japan as would plague any other government.

Discussion of authoritarianism in Japan is often linked to the militaristic period of the pre-war years. Japanese expansion in Asia at the end of the last century began in circumstances which turned out to be very favourable to such a development. They were a combination of the dynamism of Japan's modernization, carried out under the direction of a leadership with a strong military background, and the opportunity provided by the advanced decomposition of the Chinese Empire.

The postwar economic growth and expansion of Japan have been carried out in a different international environment and by a leadership which is not steeped in the military ethos, despite a certain nostalgia for some of the values which stemmed from it. Moreover, military means, which seemed so necessary to protect economic interests in the days of colonies, extraterritorial concessions, and the competition with rival imperialisms over the prostrate body of China, may no longer be very relevant for such tasks. A Japan bent on protecting its overseas interests at the end of this century may seek to do so with other instruments : the manipulation of multinational companies, or investment and trading policies, or even a Japanese version of the CIA. A new military expansion seems most unlikely.

On the specific question of relations with China, it is reasonable to suppose that no Japanese government, whatever its political complexion, would wish to try to impose its policy by military force.

Developments within China

After a quarter of a century under the rule of the original leaders of the revolution, the People's Republic of China entered a transitional period in the mid-1970s. At that time, discussions of China's future turned around the examination of at least three models. In the first, a collective leadership pursues moderate policies at home and abroad, although the voices of radicalism may be loud. In the second, a revolutionary leadership seeks to strike a radical posture in domestic and international politics. In the third, there is a period of internal disorder arising out of a power struggle at the centre and between it and regional or provincial governments, leading to disintegration and possible fragmentation of the state.

The events of the autumn of 1976 marked the downfall of the so-called 'radical' element in the Party, and, at least for the time being, removed model two from our calculations. It seems that the Chinese people are tired of living in a revolutionary ferment and long for a period of orderly development. Whether this means that the government will not have a 'radical voice' is more doubtful. It is perhaps significant that Chiang Ch'ing and her companions have been accused of following the capitalist road under the guise of their radicalism – an accusation also levelled against Lin Piao in 1971. It may be that the revolutionary message of Mao has become the orthodoxy in the name of which all policies have to be justified, even though they bear little resemblance to the policies he might have advocated.

In spite of an outward display of unity around the new leadership under Hua Kuo-feng, the third model cannot be ruled out entirely, especially as the aftermath of the Cultural Revolution revealed a tendency towards regionalism under military leadership. Furthermore, it is widely believed that the People's Liberation Army played an important part in the power struggle of 1976. China has always been prone to fissiparous tendencies. The sheer size and the geography of the country make it difficult for the central government to keep a firm hold over outlying provinces and regions, many of which have substantial ethnic minorities with links to populations beyond China's borders. None the less, the ability of the Peking government to hold the country together and reassert control in outlying territories during the past twenty-seven years in spite of economic crises, the turmoil of the Cultural Revolution, the power struggle of the mid-1970s, and the existence of a rival régime on Taiwan, suggests that there is a very good chance of China's survival as a unified state. This prospect is strengthened by the deliberate cultivation over the past quarter-century of the people's national consciousness, based on an ideological system.

The course of Chinese policy will depend on the relative strengths of party, army, and the state bureaucracy. The balance between the central government and the regional authorities could be even more important. A government struggling to maintain control over the whole country might try to strengthen its hold by encouraging xenophobia and insulating the country from much contact with the outside world, while maintaining a high degree of verbal hostility towards it. A government more sure of its authority could be expected to widen contacts with other countries.

In speculating about the future, we can be fairly certain of several constants in Chinese policy. It will place a premium on national unity. It will aim at stability and economic growth, although the debate over means will be conducted in a marxist idiom. Thirdly, foreign economic interests will not be allowed to acquire influence over the shaping of the national economy, however much China depends on the import of technology and capital goods. Lastly, while China is unlikely to be expansionist, it will try to curb the influence of its more powerful neighbours – the Soviet Union now and, perhaps, Japan in the late 1980s – by supporting countervailing forces in the region, such as nationalist revolutionary movements, and in other parts of the world.

The Evolution of the International Environment

The Sino-Soviet confrontation presents the most threatening aspect of the international scene in northeast Asia, although tensions in Korea might quickly escalate into open conflict between North and South. However, the interests of the four major powers in the peninsula guarantee a certain restraint on the part of each which would ensure that this remained a localized conflict. The dangers of the Sino-Soviet conflict lie in the fact that this is a direct confrontation of two great states with a long common frontier.

The most recent indications are that the United States, China, and Japan may draw together in a common policy of blocking Soviet expansion into the Pacific. For the reasons discussed in the preceding chapter, Japan will be anxious to avoid any confrontation which pits her military forces against those of the Soviet Union. Instead, she will hope to fend off pressures through the development of efficient maritime and air defences and a reliance on the support of the United States and China.

A less stark prognosis of the international situation would suggest that the principal feature to emerge from the confused and rapidly changing international scene is the web of common and conflicting interests which links the major states of the region. No one set of relationships is absolutely hostile – not even that of the Soviet Union and China – and no one set of relationships is wholly co-operative.

This may be illustrated if we take Japan as the focal point of our analysis. The United States has an interest in maintaining its treaty with Japan. It provides a means of inhibiting any Japanese inclination to move closer to one of the other major powers and of controlling any tendency for Japan to expand militarily. This latter objective is shared by China.

The Chinese have a complex set of motives in dealing with Japan. They wish to tap the resources of the Japanese economy without, however, allowing the Japanese to penetrate the Chinese economy. They want to prevent any collusion between Japan and the Soviet Union, an aim shared by the United States, or any closer co-operation than exists at present between Japan and the United States, an aim shared by the Soviet Union. Above all, they oppose any tendency of the Japanese to dominate South Korea or countries in Southeast Asia.

Soviet policy, too, seeks to tap the resources of Japanese capital and technology. It tries to prevent any close collaboration between the Chinese and Japanese, an objective shared to some extent by the United States. Finally, the Russians seek to draw Japan into their orbit. In pursuit of this objective they dangle the bait of Siberian riches and a more accommodating position over the territorial issue, or utter dark and vague threats about the consequences of Japan's 'unfriendly' attitude.

In brief, all the major powers wish to use Japan but simultaneously suspect it. The converse is also true. Japan is attracted to and suspicious of all the other powers.

Besides providing a guarantee against pressures and threats from the Soviet Union and China, the United States is also economically attractive. At the same time it is an economic competitor and is becoming more so as it joins the ranks of the major oil-importing countries. From the Japanese point of view, its diplomacy has also become unreliable. The end of rigid confrontation with the communist states and the development of intricate relationships with Russia and China has changed Japan's geopolitical position. It is no longer a bastion facing a solid communist front on the Asian mainland, but has become an important actor in a confused international scene in which all the other actors could be friends or enemies or, more likely, something of both.

China, too, is economically attractive and its pull is strengthened by sentimental attachments – which may, however, be weakening as the postwar generation assumes the leadership of Japan. The element of competition is also present and is complicated by uncertainty over developments in Taiwan. Finally, the dominant élites are fearful of the ideological impact that China may exercise on Japan, particularly when that impact is allied to an emotional view of China.

If public feelings about China are, on balance, inclined to be more sympathetic than hostile, the opposite is true of feelings about the Soviet Union. Here, too, there are obvious economic advantages in a closer relationship, and some strategic analysts favour a *rapprochement* with the Soviet Union as a counter to the uncertainties of Chinese and American policies. Nevertheless, territorial claims, fear of Russian ambitions in Asia, and deep-rooted suspicions and hostility are formidable if not insuperable obstacles in the way of a more formal Soviet-Japanese association.

The Japanese will probably try to adjust to the complexities of the international environment in east Asia by pursuing a line of studied ambiguity, with the object of keeping open as many options as possible in dealings with their two great continental neighbours. Behind it lies the conviction that Japan should not become deeply involved on the Asian mainland – a conviction born out of the experience of the past and the realities of today.

CONCLUSION

A chapter in Japan's relations with China had come to an end in 1949, although it took another generation before one could speak of a new one. It had opened in the last quarter of the nineteenth century and was closed in two stages : 1945 witnessed the end of Japan's militant expansion; 1949 saw the end of China's political weakness. The next two decades were a period when each country was primarily inward-looking, coming to terms with its own condition and circumstances.

During this period Japan's relations with China were both difficult and peripheral to its main concerns : economic reconstruction and adjustment to an international situation over which the Japanese had very little influence and in which they depended on the United States for their external security. However, the China problem could not be ignored because it was at the centre of international politics in east

Asia and thus occupied an important place in the debate over foreign policy.

It is not correct to depict this period as one in which Japan's only policy was that of following the American lead. Instead, there emerges a picture of the search for an adjustment to the new realities of China – an adjustment that had to be independent of American policy. The distinctive Japanese approach was noticeable from the start in the continuous efforts to develop relations with the Mainland. The absence of a formal diplomatic framework for these relations made them no less real, for the blurring of distinctions between the 'official' and the 'unofficial' is not new in the long history of the relationship with China.[13]

The relationship turned around a number of specific issues, which included the linkage between China policy and nationalist sentiment in Japan. However, as time went on, it became clearer that these issues would no longer occupy the central place in Japanese policy that the China question had held before the war. This was, of course, due to the changes which had taken place in Japan, in China, and in the international environment.

Perhaps the most important change was the elimination of the military, though not the security, factor from Japanese policy and it will not have escaped notice that the discussion in this chapter has tended to dismiss the possibility of a massive Japanese rearmament. It remains a possibility and there is no doubt that Japan has the capacity to mount a formidable military effort, both conventional and nuclear. However, the changes that have taken place in Japan and in the international environment make it the least likely of Japan's options. The risk that such a policy would entail in terms of domestic and international stability would seem to outweigh any benefits that might be gained.

On the other hand, the development of a minimal nuclear deterrent on the French model is seen as more feasible. It might look particularly attractive if the United States were to withdraw its military presence from Japan. However, the reversal of one of the most basic and constantly proclaimed policies of the past thirty years – not to acquire nuclear weapons – and the likely domestic and foreign reaction to it, would again make this a most hazardous course for any government to follow.

A point that emerges clearly is that to consider Japan's relations with China in terms of total confrontation or of intimate collaboration is to paint pictures of possible but not probable futures. Moreover, they reflect views that are influenced by the experience of the past century, which was only a short interlude in the long history of Japan's adjustment to China. The likelihood is of a much more complex relationship which moves back and forth along the spectrum between the two extremes.

Dramatic changes in Japan would not necessarily be followed by a movement to either extreme. Only the collapse of China with the consequence of large areas falling under Soviet domination, or the outbreak of war between China and Russia might provoke a rapid reorientation of Japanese policy. I have suggested that these are remote contingencies, but if they were to come about, Japan would try to seek security in a close association with the United States and other Pacific countries, including Canada, Australia, New Zealand, and possibly some in Southeast Asia, for example the Philippines and Indonesia, with the object of preventing Russia from dominating east Asia and the western Pacific. At the worst, the east Asian mainland might have to be written off, but never the western Pacific.

In both eventualities – Chinese collapse or Sino-Soviet war – the threat would be seen as coming from the Soviet Union. The prospect of China's becoming an economic and military giant, threatening to dominate the whole region, lies in the more distant future. In the meanwhile, in the context of an international system which includes Soviet and American involvement in east Asia, Japan seems to be working towards business-like but friendly relations with China (although it seems that a very close association is not the objective).

Such a policy would appear to carry most hope for the future of the region. Furthermore, it would be in harmony with Japan's basic concerns, for it would enable Japan to reconcile the demands of its global economic interests with the need to adjust to the conflicting pressures of the regional environment.

NOTES

1 Examples of the confrontation model may be found in Donald C. Hellmann, *Japan and East Asia: the New International Order* (London, Pall Mall Press, 1972) and John E. Endicott, *Japan's Nuclear Option: Political, Technical, and Strategic Factors* (New York, Praeger, 1975). In a vigorously argued thesis, Hellmann concludes that the two countries are heading for confrontation within the East and Southeast Asian international sub-system. Endicott makes no such prognostications. However, his examination of Japan's nuclear option leads him to take a military view of international relations which stresses the adversary relationship between states. Thus his book assumes that China is one of Japan's potential enemies, although he concludes that Japan is unlikely to meet the 'threat' by developing its own nuclear armament.

2 An interesting example of this model is to be found in an article by

Johan Galtung, 'Japan and Future World Politics', *Journal of Peace Research*, 1973, no. 4, pp. 355–85.

3   One of the most notable exponents of this view is Herman Kahn, *The Emerging Japanese Superstate: Challenge and Response* (Englewood Cliffs, NJ, Prentice-Hall, 1970). A more recent statement of the thesis is Norman Macrae's feature article in *The Economist*, 4 Jan 1975, pp. 15–35, entitled 'Pacific Century, 1975–2075?' This model is principally based on extrapolations of contemporary economic trends.

4   This is essentially Macrae's thesis as expounded in his article cited in n. 3 above.

5   Tsuru Shigeto, *The Mainsprings of Japanese Growth: a Turning Point?* (Paris, The Atlantic Institute for International Affairs, Feb 1977).

6   Although the Chinese navy is being modernized and has an increasing submarine component, it is essentially a defensive force. See *The Military Balance 1976–1977* (London, International Institute for Strategic Studies, 1976), pp. 49–51.

7   The evidence first came to light with the Mitsuya (Operation Three Arrows) Plan in 1965, which laid down procedures of dubious legality and indicated that Japanese strategy envisaged the possibility of military operations in and around Korea. A recent example concerns the existence of a document prepared by the National Defence Agency and subsequently withdrawn under pressure coming from the Diet. According to the document, Japan was to have considered taking over some of the American defence burden by increasing its 'non-project economic aid', which would have augmented South Korea's capacity for military spending. Military staff talks between Japan and South Korea have also been known to take place periodically.

8   *Strategic Survey 1974* (London, International Institute for Strategic Studies, 1975), pp. 34–8.

9   For a discussion of the capabilities and potential of China's nuclear weapons and their possible impact on the strategic balance in the Far East, see H. Gelber, *Nuclear Weapons and Chinese Policy* (London, International Institute for Strategic Studies, Adelphi Paper 99, Summer 1973), especially pp. 17–33.

10 The question of Japanese perceptions of the world is closely bound up with discussion of the social psychology of the Japanese, which has spawned a vast literature. The search for 'identity' was responsible for more than forty books in 1972 alone ('Why the search for Identity?', editorial, *The Japan Interpreter*, vol. VIII, no. 2, Spring 1973, pp. 153–8; also, Minami Hiroshi, 'The Introspection Boom: Whither the National Character', ibid., pp. 159–75). The Bibliographical Note, below, includes works in English which deal with these problems.

11 See the very interesting article by Ronald Dore, 'The Prestige Factor in International Affairs' (*International Affairs*, Apr 1975, pp. 190–207), which not only deals with this much neglected aspect of the study of international relations but also includes insights into the values which the Japanese bring to the conduct of international relations.

12 See John K. Fairbank, ed., *The Chinese World Order: Traditional*

China's Foreign Relations (Cambridge, Mass., Harvard UP, 1968), especially 'Preliminary Framework' by Fairbank and "The Chinese Perception of World Order, Past and Present' by Benjamin Schwartz. See also, M. Frederick Nelson, *Korea and the Old Orders in Eastern Asia* (Baton Rouge, Louisiana State UP, 1946), pp. 14–19, 78–80, 86–106. There is a neat little description of the concept of hegemony in east Asian international relations, in Lincoln Li, *The Japanese Army in North China, 1937–1941: Problems of Political and Economic Control* (Tokyo, OUP, 1975), pp. 19–22.

13 For early examples of the 'separation of politics from economics', of the connection between the 'official' and the 'unofficial', and of the exploitation of relations with China for domestic political purposes, see George Sansom, *A History of Japan*, vol. I: *To 1334*, pp. 422–3, and vol. II: *1334–1615*, pp. 167–77 (London, The Cresset Press, 1958 and 1961 respectively).

Tables

TABLE I Japan's Trade with China 1952–1976
(US $ million)

Year	Total Trade*	Imports	Exports	Balance*
1952	15·5	14·9	0·6	−14·3
1953	34·2	29·7	4·5	−25·2
1954	59·9	40·8	19·1	−21·7
1955	109·4	80·8	28·6	−52·2
1956	151·0	83·7	67·3	−16·4
1957	141·0	80·5	60·5	−20·0
1958	105·0	54·4	50·6	−3·8
1959	22·6	18·9	3·7	−15·2
1960	23·4	20·7	2·7	−18·0
1961	47·6	30·9	16·7	−14·2
1962	84·5	46·0	38·5	−7·5
1963	137·0	74·6	62·4	−12·2
1964	310·5	157·8	152·7	−5·1
1965	470·0	224·7	245·3	+20·6
1966	621·4	306·2	315·2	+9·0
1967	557·8	269·5	288·3	+18·8
1968	549·7	224·2	325·5	+101·3
1969	625·4	234·6	390·8	+156·2
1970	822·7	253·8	568·9	+315·1
1971	901·8	323·3	578·5	+255·2
1972	1,100·8	491·1	609·7	+118·6
1973	2,016·0	974·0	1,042·0	+68·0
1974	3,287·0	1,304·0	1,983·0	+679·0
1975	3,787·6	1,529·4	2,258·2	+728·8
1976	3,038·5	1,372·7	1,665·8	+293·1

* Compiled by the author.

Sources: For the years 1952–4, Direction of International Trade, UN Statistical Office [1956]; for 1955–7, ibid. 1958; for 1958–62, Direction of Trade, IMF and IBRD [1964?]; for 1963–7, ibid. [1969?]; for 1968–72, ibid. [1973?]; for 1973–5, ibid., IMF [1976]; for 1976, ibid., Mar 1977.

TABLE II
Total Japan-China Trade and L-T (MT) and Friendly Trade
1963–1971 (Unit: $1000)

Year	Total Volume of Foreign Trade (1)	L-T (MT) Trade (2)	Friendly Trade (3)
1963	137,016	64,115 (46·7%)	72,901 (53·3%)
1964	310,489	128,427 (41·1%)	182,026 (58·6%)
1965	469,741	179,186 (38·1%)	290,555 (61·9%)
1966	621,387	205,228 (33·0%)	416,159 (67·0%)
1967	557,733	153,483 (27·5%)	404,250 (72·5%)
1968	549,623	115,920 (21·1%)	433,703 (78·9%)
1969	625,343	69,600 (11·7%)	555,743 (88·9%)
1970	822,696	70,000 (8·5%)	752,696 (91·5%)
1971	900,000	84,220 (9·1%)	815,780 (90·9%)

Note: (1) The total volume of foreign trade is based on the customs clearance basis.
  (2) L-T (1963–7) and MT (1968–70) trade are estimates based on the contract basis.
  (3) Friendly trade: (1)–(2).

Source: Japan External Trade Organization, *How to Approach the China Market* (Tokyo, Press International, 1972), p. 131.

Present author's note: It is assumed that the unit is US $1000, and that the second column of the table refess to the total volume of trade with China.

TABLE III   Exchange of Persons between Japan and China 1949–1973

Year	Japanese visiting China		Chinese visiting Japan
1949	6		0
1950	0		0
1951	9		0
1952	50		0
1953	139		0
1954	192		10
			30 Oct. Visit of the first Communist delegation: the Chinese Red Cross Society to receive thanks from Japanese Red Cross for facilitating repatriation of Japanese
1955	847 ⎫	Topped the list	100
1956	1,182 ⎬	of foreign	142
	⎭	tourists	
1957	1,243		140
1958	594		93
1959	191		0
1960	629		13
1961	537		85
1962	619		78
1963	1,752		280
1964	1,844		489
1965	3,806		397
1966	2,250		356
1967	2,189		57
1968	2,304		4
1969	2,463		7
1970	n.a.		n.a.
1971	c. 3,200		71
1972	c. 8,000		537
1973	10,238		1,991

n.a. Figures not available to the author.

Sources: New China Almanac: 1970 (quoted in *Tōyō Keizai*, special issue on the Chinese economy, 22 Oct 1971, p. 172); Shao-chuan Leng, *Japan and Communist China* (Kyoto, Dōshisha University Press, 1958), pp. 20, 75; Fukui Haruhiro, *Party In Power* (Berkeley, University of California Press, 1970), pp. 227–40; *Japan Times Weekly*, 5 May 1973; Hirasawa Kazushige, 'Japan's Emerging Foreign Policy', *Foreign Affairs*, Oct 1975, p. 156.

TABLE IV   Japan's Trade with Taiwan 1952–1976
(US $ million)

Year	Total Trade*	Imports	Exports	Balance*
1952	124·3	63·7	60·6	−3·1
1953	124·9	64·0	60·9	−3·1
1954	123·0	57·1	65·9	+8·8
1955	144·7	80·9	63·8	−17·1
1956	123·4	45·5	77·9	+32·4
1957	151·6	67·3	84·3	+17·0
1958	165·6	75·6	90·0	+14·4
1959	158·5	71·6	86·9	+15·3
1960	165·8	63·5	102·3	+38·8
1961	163·9	67·6	96·3	+28·7
1962	179·9	61·4	118·5	+57·1
1963	229·7	122·6	107·1	−15·5
1964	279·5	141·3	138·2	−3·1
1965	375·3	157·4	217·9	+60·5
1966	402·8	147·4	255·4	+108·0
1967	465·3	137·1	328·2	+191·1
1968	622·4	150·7	471·7	+321·0
1969	786·9	180·5	606·4	+425·9
1970	951·2	250·8	700·4	+449·6
1971	1,210·0	284·9	925·1	+640·2
1972	1,514·1	421·7	1,092·4	+670·7
1973	2,537·0	892·0	1,645·0	+753·0
1974	2,962·0	954·0	2,008·0	+1,054·0
1975	2,630·8	811·0	1,819·8	+1,008·8
1976	3,474·7	1,191·7	2,283·0	+1,091·3

* Compiled by the author.

Sources: For the years 1952–4, *Direction of International Trade*, UN Statistical Office [1956]; for 1955–7, ibid. 1958; for 1958–62, *Direction of Trade*, IMF and IBRD [1964?]; for 1963–7, ibid. [1969?]; for 1968–72, ibid. [1973?]; for 1973–5, ibid., IMF [1976]; for 1976, ibid., Mar 1977.

TABLE V Japan's Exports and Imports by Principal Areas 1968–1976 (Customs Clearance Basis, US$ million)

	1968	1969	1970	1971	1972	1973	1974	1975	1976	Component Ratio
Exports										
Developed Area	6,746 (27.4)	8,331 (23.5)	10,440 (25.3)	13,027 (24.8)	15,959 (22.5)	19,046 (19.3)	26,421 (38.7)	23,434 (−11.3)	31,620 (34.9)	47.0
USA	4,086 (35.7)	4,958 (21.3)	5,940 (19.8)	7,495 (26.2)	8,848 (18.1)	9,449 (6.8)	12,799 (35.5)	11,149 (−12.9)	15,690 (40.7)	23.3
Western Europe	1,659 (16.0)	2,059 (24.1)	2,905 (41.1)	3,395 (16.9)	4,749 (39.9)	6,543 (37.8)	8,593 (31.3)	8,131 (−5.4)	10,946 (34.6)	16.3
EC (EEC) (1)	687 (25.8)	968 (40.9)	1,303 (34.6)	1,635 (25.5)	2,203 (34.7)	4,400 (99.7)	5,968 (35.6)	5,675 (−4.9)	7,234 (27.5)	10.8
Developing Area	5,640 (22.1)	6,888 (22.1)	7,827 (13.6)	9,834 (25.6)	11,187 (13.8)	15,929 (42.4)	25,187 (58.1)	27,632 (9.7)	30,926 (11.9)	46.0
South East Asia	3,613 (23.3)	4,448 (23.1)	4,902 (10.2)	5,763 (17.6)	6,310 (9.5)	8,931 (41.5)	12,695 (42.1)	12,543 (−1.2)	14,047 (12.0)	20.9
Middle East	535 (34.4)	627 (17.2)	634 (1.1)	824 (30.0)	1,174 (42.5)	1,774 (51.1)	3,680 (107.4)	6,075 (65.1)	7,276 (19.8)	10.8
Communist Bloc	582 (10.9)	764 (31.3)	1,045 (36.8)	1,148 (9.9)	1,442 (25.6)	1,954 (35.5)	3,927 (101.0)	4,683 (19.3)	4,679 (−0.1)	7.0
Total (2)	12,972 (24.2)	15,990 (23.3)	19,318 (20.8)	24,019 (24.3)	28,591 (19.0)	36,930 (29.2)	55,536 (50.4)	55,753 (0.4)	67,225 (20.6)	100.0
Imports										
Developed Area	6,865 (10.4)	7,912 (15.3)	10,430 (31.8)	10,277 (−1.5)	12,332 (20.0)	19,785 (60.4)	25,782 (30.3)	23,894 (−7.3)	26,049 (9.0)	40.2
USA	3,527 (9.8)	4,090 (16.0)	5,560 (35.9)	4,978 (−10.5)	5,852 (17.6)	9,270 (58.4)	12,682 (36.8)	11,608 (−8.5)	11,809 (1.7)	18.2
Western Europe	1,301 (8.1)	1,492 (14.7)	1,962 (31.5)	2,062 (5.1)	2,479 (20.2)	4,066 (64.0)	5,234 (28.7)	4,395 (−16.0)	4,957 (12.8)	7.6
EC (EEC) (1)	737 (12.5)	821 (11.4)	1,117 (36.1)	1,138 (1.9)	1,395 (22.6)	3,177 (127.7)	3,982 (25.3)	3,371 (−15.3)	3,623 (7.5)	5.6
Developing Area	5,283 (15.5)	6,263 (18.6)	7,564 (20.8)	8,490 (12.2)	9,912 (16.7)	16,242 (63.9)	33,174 (104.2)	30,962 (−6.7)	35,897 (15.9)	55.4
South East Asia	1,984 (10.5)	2,381 (20.0)	3,013 (26.5)	3,404 (13.0)	4,171 (22.5)	7,953 (90.7)	12,497 (57.1)	10,586 (−15.3)	13,411 (26.7)	20.7
Middle East	1,817 (19.3)	1,989 (9.5)	2,337 (17.5)	3,013 (28.9)	3,491 (15.9)	4,941 (41.5)	15,920 (222.2)	16,477 (3.5)	18,745 (13.8)	28.9
Communist Bloc	837 (−3.6)	848 (15.7)	887 (4.6)	944 (6.4)	1,226 (28.9)	2,286 (86.5)	3,141 (37.4)	3,006 (−4.3)	2,845 (−5.3)	4.4
Total (2)	12,987 (11.4)	15,024 (15.7)	18,881 (25.7)	19,712 (4.4)	23,471 (19.1)	38,314 (63.2)	62,110 (62.1)	57,863 (−6.8)	64,799 (12.0)	100.0
Balance										
Developed Area	−119	419	10	2,750	3,627	−739	639	−460	5,571	
USA	559	868	380	2,517	2,996	179	117	−459	3,881	
Western Europe	358	567	943	1,333	2,270	2,477	3,359	3,736	5,989	
EC (EEC) (1)	−50	147	186	497	808	1,223	1,986	2,304	3,611	
Developing Area	357	625	263	1,344	1,275	−313	−7,987	−3,330	−4,971	
South East Asia	1,629	2,067	1,889	2,359	2,139	978	198	1,957	636	
Middle East	−1,282	−1,362	−1,703	−2,189	−2,317	−3,167	−12,240	−10,402	−11,469	
Communist Bloc	−255	−84	158	204	216	−332	786	1,677	1,833	
Total (2)	−15	966	437	4,307	5,120	−1,384	−6,574	−2,110	2,426	

Notes: (1) From 1973, including exports to or imports from Denmark, United Kingdom and Ireland.
(2) Including exports to or imports from unidentified areas.
(3) Figures in parentheses denote percentage change compared with the previous year.
(4) Component ratio for 1976.

Source: Compiled by the Yamaichi Research Institute of Securities & Economics, Inc, Tokyo.

Appendixes

EXCHANGE OF LETTERS BETWEEN THE JAPANESE PRIME MINISTER, MR
SHIGERU YOSHIDA, AND MR JOHN FOSTER DULLES, REGARDING JAPAN'S
POLICY TOWARDS CHINA

Mr Yoshida's letter, 24 December 1951

Dear Ambassador Dulles,
    While the Japanese Peace Treaty and the U.S.-Japan Security
Treaty were being debated in the House of Representatives and the
House of Councillors of the Diet, a number of questions were put and
statements made relative to Japan's future policy toward China. Some
of the statements, separated from their context and background, gave
rise to misapprehensions which I should like to clear up.
    The Japanese Government desires ultimately to have a full measure
of political peace and commercial intercourse with China which is
Japan's close neighbour.
    At the present time it is, we hope, possible to develop that kind of
relationship with the National Government of the Republic of China,
which has the seat, voice and vote of China in the United Nations,
which exercises actual government authority over certain territory, and
which maintains diplomatic relations with most of the members of
the United Nations. To that end my Government on November 17,
1951, established a Japanese Government Overseas Agency in Formosa,
with the consent of the National Government of China. This is the
highest form of relationship with other countries which is now permitted
to Japan, pending the coming into force of the multilateral Treaty of
Peace. The Japanese Government Overseas Agency in Formosa is
important in its personnel, reflecting the importance which my government attaches to relations with the National Government of the Republic of China. My government is prepared as soon as legally possible
to conclude with the National Government of China, if that government
so desires, a Treaty which will re-establish normal relations between the

two Governments in conformity with the principles set out in the multilateral Treaty of Peace. The terms of such bilateral treaty shall, in respect of the Republic of China, be applicable to all territories which are now, or which may hereafter be, under the control of the National Government of the Republic of China. We will promptly explore this subject with the National Government of China.

As regards the Chinese Communist regime, that regime stands actually condemned by the United Nations of being an aggressor and in consequence, the United Nations has recommended certain measures against that regime, in which Japan is now concurring and expects to continue to concur when the multilateral Treaty of Peace comes into force pursuant to the provisions of Article 5(a) (iii), whereby Japan has undertaken 'to give the United Nations every assistance in any action it takes in accordance with the Charter and to refrain from giving assistance to any State against which the United Nations may take preventive or enforcement action'. Furthermore, the Sino-Soviet Treaty of Friendship, Alliance and Mutual Assistance concluded in Moscow in 1950 is virtually a military alliance aimed against Japan. In fact there are many reasons to believe that the Communist regime in China is backing the Japan Communist Party in its program of seeking violently to overthrow the constitutional system and the present Government of Japan. In view of these considerations, I can assure you that the Japanese Government has no intention to conclude a bilateral Treaty with the Communist regime of China.

Yours sincerely,
SHIGERU YOSHIDA

Mr Dulles's reply, 16 January 1952

My dear Mr. Prime Minister,

I acknowledge the receipt by pouch of your letter of December 24, 1951, in which you express the intentions of your Government with reference to China.

This clear statement should dispel any misapprehensions which, as you suggest, may have arisen from statements, separated from their context and background, made during the course of debate in Japan on the ratification of the Japanese Peace Treaty and the U.S.-Japan Security Treaty.

I am grateful to you for your letter and I respect the courageous and forthright manner in which you face up to this difficult and controversial matter.

Sincerely yours,
JOHN FOSTER DULLES

Source: Denise Folliot, ed., *Documents on International Affairs 1952* (London, OUP for RIIA, 1955), pp. 474–5.

APPENDIX B

TREATY OF PEACE BETWEEN JAPAN AND NATIONALIST CHINA, TAIPEI, 28 APRIL 1952

Japan and the Republic of China,
Considering their mutual desire for good neighborliness in view of their historical and cultural ties and geographical proximity;
Realizing the importance of their close cooperation to the promotion of their common welfare and to the maintenance of international peace and security;
Recognizing the need of a settlement of problems that have arisen as a result of the existence of a state of war between them;
Have resolved to conclude a Treaty of Peace and have accordingly appointed as their Plenipotentiaries,
The Government of Japan :
Mr. Isao Kawada;
His Excellency the President of the Republic of China :
Mr. Yeh Kung Chao;
Who, having communicated to each other their full powers found to be in good and due form, have agreed upon the following articles :

ARTICLE I

The state of war between Japan and the Republic of China is terminated as from the date on which the present Treaty enters into force.

ARTICLE II

It is recognized that under Article 2 of the Treaty of Peace with Japan signed at the city of San Francisco in the United States of America on September 8, 1951 (hereinafter referred to as the San Francisco Treaty), Japan has renounced all right, title and claim to Taiwan (Formosa) and Penghu (the Pescadores) as well as the Spratly Islands and the Paracel Islands.

ARTICLE III

The disposition of property of Japan and its nationals in Taiwan (Formosa) and Penghu (the Pescadores), and their claims, including debts, against the authorities of the Republic of China in Taiwan (Formosa) and Penghu (the Pescadores) and the residents thereof, and the disposition in Japan of property of such authorities and residents and their claims, including debts, against Japan and its nationals, shall be the subject of special arrangements between the Government of Japan and the Government of the Republic of China. The terms nationals and residents whenever used in the present Treaty include juridical persons.

ARTICLE IV

It is recognized that all treaties, conventions and agreements concluded before December 9, 1941, between Japan and China have become null and void as a consequence of the war.

ARTICLE V

It is recognized that under the provisions of Article 10 of the San Francisco Treaty, Japan has renounced all special rights and interests in China, including all benefits and privileges resulting from the provisions of the final Protocol signed at Peking on September 7, 1901, and all annexes, notes and documents supplementary thereto, and has agreed to the abrogation in respect to Japan of the said protocol, annexes, notes and documents.

ARTICLE VI

(*a*) Japan and the Republic of China will be guided by the principles of Article 2 of the Charter of the United Nations in their mutual relations.

(*b*) Japan and the Republic of China will cooperate in accordance with the principles of the Charter of the United Nations and, in particular, will promote their common welfare through friendly cooperation in the economic field.

ARTICLE VII

Japan and the Republic of China will endeavour to conclude, as soon as possible, a treaty or agreement to place their trading, maritime and other commercial relations on a stable and friendly basis.

ARTICLE VIII

Japan and the Republic of China will endeavour to conclude, as soon as possible, an agreement relating to civil air transport.

ARTICLE IX

Japan and the Republic of China will endeavour to conclude, as soon as possible, an agreement providing for the regulation or limitation of fishing and the conservation and development of fisheries on the high seas.

ARTICLE X

For the purpose of the present Treaty, nationals of the Republic of China shall be deemed to include all the inhabitants and former inhabitants of Taiwan (Formosa) and Penghu (the Pescadores) and their descendants who are of the Chinese nationality in accordance with the laws and regulations which have been or may hereafter be enforced by the Republic of China in Taiwan (Formosa) and Penghu (the Pescadores); and juridical persons of the Republic of China shall be deemed to include all those registered under the laws and regulations which have been or may hereafter be enforced by the Republic of China in Taiwan (Formosa) and Penghu (the Pescadores).

ARTICLE XI

Unless otherwise provided for in the present Treaty and the documents supplementary thereto, any problem arising between Japan and the Republic of China as a result of the existence of a state of war shall be settled in accordance with the relevant provisions of the San Francisco Treaty.

ARTICLE XII

Any dispute that may arise out of the interpretation on application of the present Treaty shall be settled by negotiation or by other pacific means.

ARTICLE XIII

The present Treaty shall be ratified and the instruments of ratification shall be exchanged at Taipei as soon as possible. The present Treaty shall enter into force as from the date on which such instruments of ratification are exchanged.

ARTICLE XIV

The present Treaty shall be in the Japanese, Chinese and English languages. In case of any divergence of interpretation, the English text shall prevail.

IN WITNESS WHEREOF, the respective Plenipotentiaries have signed the present Treaty and have affixed thereto their seals.

Done in duplicate at Taipei, this 28th day of the fourth month of the Twenty Seventh year of Showa of Japan corresponding to the 28th day of the fourth month of the Forty First year of the Republic of China and to the 28th day of April in the year One Thousand Nine Hundred and Fifty Two.

For Japan : (signed) ISAO KAWADA
For the Republic of China : (signed) YEH KUNG CHAO

PROTOCOL

At the moment of signing this day the Treaty of Peace between Japan and the Republic of China (hereinafter referred to as the present Treaty), the undersigned Plenipotentiaries have agreed upon the following terms which shall constitute an integral part of the present Treaty :

1. The application of Article XI of the present Treaty shall be subject to the following understandings :

(*a*) Wherever a period is stipulated in the San Francisco Treaty during which Japan assumes an obligation or undertaking, such period shall, in respect of any part of the territories of the Republic of China, commence immediately when the present Treaty becomes applicable to such part of the territories.

(*b*) As a sign of magnanimity and good will towards the Japanese people, the Republic of China voluntarily waives the benefit of the services to be made available by Japan pursuant to Article 14(a) of the San Francisco Treaty.

(*c*) Articles 11 and 18 of the San Francisco Treaty shall be excluded from the operation of Article XI of the present Treaty.

2. The commerce and navigation between Japan and the Republic of China shall be governed by the following Arrangements :

(*a*) Each Party will mutually accord to nationals, products and vessels of the other Party :

(i) Most-favored-nation treatment with respect to customs duties, charges, restrictions and other regulations on or in connection with the importation and exportation of goods; and

(ii) Most-favored-nation treatment with respect to shipping, navigation and imported goods, and with respect to natural and juridical persons and their interests – such treatment to include all matters pertaining to the levying and collection of taxes, access to the courts, the making and performance of contracts, rights to property (including those relating to intangible property and excluding those with respect to mining), participation in juridical entities, and generally the conduct of all kinds of business and professional activities with the exception of financial (including insurance) activities and those reserved by either Party exclusive to its nationals.

(*b*) Whenever the grant of most-favored-nation treatment by either Party to the other Party, concerning rights to property, participation in juridical entities and conduct of business and professional activities, as specified in sub-paragraph (*a*)(ii) of this paragraph, amounts in effect to the grant of national treatment, such Party shall not be obliged to grant more favorable treatment than that granted by the other Party under most-favored-nation treatment.

(c) External purchases and sales of government trading enterprises shall be based solely on commercial considerations.

(d) In the application of the present arrangements, it is understood :

(i) that vessels of the Republic of China shall be deemed to include all those registered under the laws and regulations which have been or may hereafter be enforced by the Republic of China in Taiwan (Formosa) and Penghu (the Pescadores); and products of the Republic of China shall be deemed to include all those originating in Taiwan (Formosa) and Penghu (the Pescadores); and

(ii) that a discriminatory measure shall not be considered to derogate from the grant of treatments prescribed above, if such measure is based on an exception customarily provided for in the commercial treaties of the Party applying it, or on the need to safeguard that Party's external financial position or balance of payments (except in respect to shipping and navigation), or on the need to maintain its essential security interests, and provided such measure is proportionate to the circumstances and not applied in an arbitrary or unreasonable manner.

The Arrangements set forth in this paragraph 2 shall remain in force for a period of one year as from the date on which the present Treaty enters into force.

Done in duplicate at Taipei, this 28th day of the fourth month of the Twenty Seventh year of Showa of Japan corresponding to the 28th day of the fourth month of the Forty First year of the Republic of China and the 28th day of April in the year One Thousand Nine Hundred and Fifty Two.

Source: Denise Folliot, ed., *Documents on International Affairs 1952* (London, OUP for RIIA, 1955), pp. 476–80.

UNIFIED VIEW OF THE FOREIGN MINISTRY CONCERNING THE CHINA PROBLEM
1964

1. *Basic Policy towards China*

The Government thinks that the most realistic policy and the one best adapted to our national interest is to maintain the existing relationships, i.e. trade with mainland China on the basis of the separation of politics from economics whilst maintaining regular diplomatic relations with the Nationalist Government. The present situation, in which both the Nationalist Government and Communist China are antagonistic to each other by insisting on their sovereignty over the whole of China, cannot be said to be a normal condition. However, our country alone does not have the power to normalize the situation. We do not think it would contribute to peace in Asia if our country severed relations with the Nationalist Government and recognized the Communist Chinese régime.

Therefore, there is no other way of finding a just solution to this problem than through thorough discussion within the UN in conformity with world opinion, and the Government will follow this policy.

2. *Possibility of Invasion by Communist China*

It is meaningless to define conceptually whether Communist China is bellicose or peace-loving. Rather, it is important to keep Communist China's intentions and concrete policy towards Asia and Japan under constant review. We think it is a fact that every country in the world fears, although in varying degrees, not only that the Communist Chinese régime wants ultimately to turn the whole world to communism, but also the danger of its expansion beyond its borders (not only in military terms, but also ideologically, politically, and economically).

At present, Communist China takes a prudent attitude towards the outside world and it is unthinkable that it will take direct military action over the Sino-Indian border, Korea, the Strait of Taiwan, Laos, Vietnam, etc. for the time being.

It is unthinkable, too, at this stage that it intends to invade our country directly with military forces. However, in addition to the aforementioned considerations, it is an important problem whether our country is capable of preventing an invasion, and, needless to say, the maintenance of our country's security is due to the existence of the Japan-US security system.

Therefore, it is wrong to assume that our country's security will be maintained even if it were disarmed and neutral. It is a well-known fact that Communist China strongly holds the view that American imperialism is the common enemy of Japan and China, but it is obvious that Communist China aims at breaking up the Japan-US security system by separating Japan from the US.

The Government will maintain contact with mainland China persistently on the basis of the separation of politics from economics. However, it is natural to think that Communist China would try to take advantage of the contact to alienate Japan from the US and Taiwan by raising a pro-China mood among the Japanese. So, needless to say, it is necessary to guard against such an ideological offensive.

3. *The Problem of Chinese Representation at the UN and the Problem of the Normalization of Diplomatic Relations with Communist China*
The problem of Chinese representation is not a simple and formal question whether the Nationalist Government or Communist China should represent China, but it is an important question related not only to the peace of Asia but to world peace. Therefore, it is our country's basic attitude that it should be discussed substantially and thoroughly and that a solution which meets world opinion should be found.

Our country will think it natural to consider the normalization of diplomatic relations with Communist China when it is proved that it is necessary and desirable for the maintenance of peace in Asia and in the world to admit Communist China to the UN, and when it is given the seat in the UN in an harmonious way, which means 'Communist China is welcomed as a rightful member of the UN'. At this stage it is too early to decide our country's concrete attitude at the UN General Assembly and we intend to be prudent, taking world opinion into consideration.

Although it is undeniable that the establishment of diplomatic relations between France and China will affect this matter, it is premature to conclude that it has had a decisive effect on the problem of Chinese representation. (Actually, it is only the Congo which has decided to recognize Communist China following the French recognition.) The basic attitude of our country remains unchanged that the issue should be discussed substantially and be given a fair solution which will be approved by world opinion.

Source: Evening edition of *Asahi*, 5 Mar 1964, reproduced in Ishikawa T. and others, eds, *Sengo Shiryō: Nicchū Kankei* (Tokyo, Nihon Hyōronsha, 1970), p. 296. Free translation made for the author by Takako Mendl.

JOINT STATEMENT OF THE GOVERNMENT OF THE PEOPLE'S REPUBLIC OF CHINA AND THE GOVERNMENT OF JAPAN

At the invitation of Premier Chou En-lai of the State Council of the People's Republic of China, Prime Minister Kakuei Tanaka of Japan visited the People's Republic of China from September 25 to 30, 1972. Accompanying Prime Minister Kakuei Tanaka were Foreign Minister Masayoshi Ohira, Chief Cabinet Secretary Susumu Nikaido and other government officials.

Chairman Mao Tsetung [*sic*] met Prime Minister Kakuei Tanaka on September 27. The two sides had an earnest and friendly conversation.

Premier Chou En-lai and Foreign Minister Chi Peng-fei had an earnest and frank exchange of views with Prime Minister Kakuei Tanaka and Foreign Minister Masayoshi Ohira, all along in a friendly atmosphere, on various matters between the two countries and other matters of interest to both sides, with the normalization of relations between China and Japan as the focal point, and the two sides agreed to issue the following joint statement of the two Governments :

China and Japan are neighbouring countries separated only by a strip of water, and there was a long history of traditional friendship between them. The two peoples ardently wish to end the abnormal state of affairs that has hitherto existed between the two countries. The termination of the state of war and the normalization of relations between China and Japan – the realization of such wishes of the two peoples will open a new page in the annals of relations between the two countries.

The Japanese side is keenly aware of Japan's responsibility for causing enormous damages in the past to the Chinese people through war and deeply reproaches itself. The Japanese side reaffirms its position that in seeking to realize the normalization of relations between Japan and China, it proceeds from the stand of fully understanding the three principles for the restoration of diplomatic relations put forward by the Government of the People's Republic of China. The Chinese side expresses its welcome for this.

Although the social systems of China and Japan are different, the two countries should and can establish peaceful and friendly relations. The normalization of relations and the development of good-neighbourly and friendly relations between the two countries are in the interests of the two peoples, and will also contribute to the relaxation of tension in Asia and the safeguarding of world peace.

(1) The abnormal state of affairs which has hitherto existed between the People's Republic of China and Japan is declared terminated on the date of publication of this statement.

(2) The Government of Japan recognizes the Government of the People's Republic of China as the sole legal government of China.

(3) The Government of the People's Republic of China reaffirms that Taiwan is an inalienable part of the territory of the People's Republic of China. The Government of Japan fully understands and respects this stand of the Government of China and adheres to its stand of complying with Article 8 of the Potsdam Proclamation.

(4) The Government of the People's Republic of China and the Government of Japan have decided upon the establishment of diplomatic relations as from September 29, 1972. The two Governments have decided to adopt all necessary measures for the establishment and performance of functions of embassies in each other's capitals in accordance with international law and practice and exchange ambassadors as speedily as possible.

(5) The Government of the People's Republic of China declares that in the interest of the friendship between the peoples of China and Japan, it renounces its demand for war indemnities from Japan.

(6) The Government of the People's Republic of China and the Government of Japan agree to establish durable relations of peace and friendship between the two countries on the basis of the principles of mutual respect for sovereignty and territorial integrity, mutual non-aggression, non-interference in each other's internal affairs, equality and mutual benefit and peaceful coexistence.

In keeping with the foregoing principles and the principles of the United Nations Charter, the Governments of the two countries affirm that in their mutual relations, all disputes shall be settled by peaceful means without resorting to the use or threat of force.

(7) The normalization of relations between China and Japan is not directed against third countries. Neither of the two countries should seek hegemony in the Asia-Pacific region and each country is opposed to efforts by any other country or group of countries to establish such hegemony.

(8) To consolidate and develop the peaceful and friendly relations between the two countries, the Government of the People's Republic of China and the Government of Japan agree to hold negotiations aimed at the conclusion of a treaty of peace and friendship.

(9) In order to further develop the relations between the two countries and broaden the exchange of visits, the Government of the People's Republic of China and the Government of Japan agree to hold negotiations aimed at the conclusion of agreements on trade,

navigation, aviation, fishery, etc., in accordance with the needs and taking into consideration the existing non-governmental agreements.

(Signed) CHOU EN-LAI
Premier of the State
Council of the People's
Republic of China

(Signed) KAKUEI TANAKA
Prime Minister of
Japan

(Signed) CHI PENG-FEI
Minister of Foreign
Affairs of the People's
Republic of China

(Signed) MASAYOSHI OHIRA
Minister for Foreign
Affairs of Japan

Peking, September 29, 1972

Source: Peking Review, vol. 15, no. 40, 6 Oct 1972, pp. 12–13.

APPENDIX E

COMPARATIVE CHRONOLOGY OF EVENTS AFFECTING JAPAN'S CHINA POLICY 1949-1976

Year	China (PRC)	Taiwan (ROC)	Japan	US/International
1949	1 Oct. Proclamation of PRC			22 Nov. Establishment of COCOM
1950	14 Feb. Sino-Soviet Treaty of Friendship, Alliance and Mutual Assistance		29 Apr. Upper House Resolution calling for trade with China	25 June. Outbreak of Korean War
	Oct. China intervenes in Korean War		Dec. SCAP imposes embargo on trade with China	
1951			24 Dec. Yoshida Letter to Dulles	8 Sep. Treaty of San Francisco and US-Japan Security Treaty signed
				26 Oct. Mutual Defense Assistance Control Act (Battle Act): US aid tied to compliance with embargo on trade with communist states

Year	China (PRC)	Japan	Taiwan (ROC)	US/International
1952			28 *Apr.* Treaty of Peace between Japan and ROC	
		End of Occupation		
	1 *June.* First unofficial Trade Agreement between Japan and PRC – barter trade system			
		Sep. Japan joins COCOM and CHINCOM		*Sep.* Establishment of CHINCOM
1953		31 *Jan.* MITI lifts ban on some items for export to China		
		29/30 *July.* Diet resolutions on trade with China		
	29 *Oct.* Second unofficial Trade Agreement between Japan and PRC			
1954		9 *Dec.* Hatoyama becomes Prime Minister		9 *Mar.* Japan-US Mutual Defence Assistance Agreement

1955	4 *May.* Third unofficial Trade Agreement between Japan and PRC	21 *June.* ROC refuses to trade with Japanese firms doing business with PRC	*April.* Bandung Conference *Aug.* Sino-American Ambassadorial talks initiated
1956	11 *Feb.* PRC proposes talks for normalization of diplomatic relations with Japan		
	Autumn. First Chinese trade fairs in Tokyo and Osaka		
	Autumn. First Japanese trade fairs in Peking and Shanghai		
	19 *Oct.* Diplomatic relations established between Japan and USSR		
	23 *Dec.* Ishibashi becomes Prime Minister		18 *Dec.* Japan enters UN
1957	25 *Feb.* Kishi becomes Prime Minister		*May.* Removal of 'China Differential' from allied trade with communist countries
	July. Embargo on trade with China reduced to COCOM level	*June.* Kishi's visit to Taiwan	

F

Year	China (PRC)	Japan	Taiwan (ROC)	US/International
1958	5 Mar. Fourth unofficial Trade Agreement between Japan and PRC		30 Mar. Kishi's letter to Chiang, reassuring him about private nature of agreements with PRC	
		Apr. Kishi tells Japanese signatories of unofficial Trade Agreement that Japan does not recognize PRC		
	10 May. Trade relations with Japan broken off	2 May. Nagasaki Flag Incident		
	Aug. Promulgation of 3 principles for Sino-Japanese relations			
1959	March. JSP/Sōhyō delegation to Peking —'Consideration Trade'			
	7 Sep. Ishibashi mission to Peking			
	Oct. Matsumura mission to Peking			

1960

May–June. Security Treaty Revision crisis

19 July, Ikeda becomes Prime Minister

27 Aug. Chou's 3 categories of Sino-Japanese trade —inauguration of 'Friendly Trade'

13 Sep. New policy towards US: embargo no longer sole barrier to trade, Taiwan issue must be settled first

1961

Spring. Japanese participation in Canton Trade Fair

15 Apr. Barter system no longer essential for trade with China

1962

May. Authorization in principle of deferred payments for steel and fertilizers in trade with PRC

Sep. Matsumura mission to Peking

9 Nov. L-T Trade Memorandum signed, covering trade for 5 years between Japan and PRC

27 Dec. Protocol signed to regulate 'Friendly Trade' between Japan and PRC

Year	China (PRC)	Japan	Taiwan (ROC)	US/International
1963	13 July. Kurashiki Rayon Co. signs contract to supply vinylon plant to PRC	20 Aug. Govt approves 5-year deferred payment plan for Kurashiki-PRC agreement 28 Aug. ROC request rejected 30 Dec. Crisis in Japan-ROC relations over Chou Hung-ching affair	22 Aug. ROC asks Japanese govt to withhold approval of the deferred payment plan 30 Oct. Ono (Vice-Pres. of LDP) mission to Taipei	Peking rebuffs US businessmen trying to participate in Canton Fair or meet Chinese trade officials in Hong Kong
1964	Jan. Chinese propose direct air service between China and Japan	Chinese proposal for air link rejected 20 Feb. Komatsu Manufacturing Co. signs largest ever contract with PRC	11 Jan. ROC suspends all new govt procurements from Japan 23–8 Feb. Yoshida visit to Taipei	19 Jan. France establishes diplomatic relations with PRC

5 *Mar.* Gaimushō publishes 'Unified View' of China problem

9 *Apr.* Matsumura visits Peking on Chou's invitation

19 *Apr.* Matsumura-Liao Agreement for exchange of journalists and trade liaison offices

Apr. Chinese trade fair in Tokyo

May. Yoshida letter to Chiang Kai-shek over deferred payments for trade with PRC

12 May. Finance Minister Tanaka announces refusal of official funds for sale of second vinylon plant by Nichibō to PRC

June. Chinese trade fair in Ōsaka

2 *July.* Govt approves PRC trade office in Tokyo, but without diplomatic status

2–5 July. Foreign Minister Ōhira visits Taipei

Year	China (PRC)	Japan	Taiwan (ROC)	US/International
	16 Oct. First Chinese nuclear explosion	9 Nov. Satō becomes Prime Minister	18 July. ROC lifts ban on govt procurements from Japan	
		21 Nov. Govt refuses entry visas for reps. from PRC, N. Korea, and N. Vietnam to attend national convention of JCP		
1965				13 Jan. Satō-Johnson talks at White House
		20 Jan. Satō at press conference: Japan will pursue independent policy towards PRC		
		21 Jan. MITI approves deferred payments for export of Nichibō plant to PRC, provided funds are raised privately	26 Jan. ROC protests against MITI decision	
	Feb. Trade Liaison Offices established in Peking and Tokyo			

15 Feb. PRC cancels provisional agreement with Tōyō Engineering Co. for urea plant because of Japan's 'unfriendly attitude'

6 Apr. PRC cancels contract with Hitachi for a freighter because Japanese govt allows ROC interference in Japan-PRC trade

19 Apr. Kawashima (Vice-Pres. of LDP) meets Chou in Djakarta

7 May. PRC cancels contract with Nichibō because of Satō govt's 'hostile attitude'

22 June. Japan-ROK Treaty and Agreements normalizing relations

2/3 Aug. Miki and Satō state that Yoshida Letter to Chiang was private and not binding on govt

Year	China (PRC)	Japan	Taiwan (ROC)	US/International
1966	28 Aug. Kosaka (former For. Min.) leads LDP mission on 4-week visit to PRC			12 Feb. Wm Bundy, US Ass. Sec. of State for Far Eastern Affairs, says US not opposed to limited exchange of persons with PRC, but Chinese response is negative
1967	10 Sep. PRC expels *Mainichi, Sankei*, and *Nishi Nippon* correspondents 31 Dec. L-T Trade Agreement expires	27 Nov. Chiang Ching-kuo visits Tokyo	7–9 Sep. Satō visit to Taiwan	
1968	22 Feb. L-T Trade Agreement extended for one year (becomes MT)	16 Apr. For. Min. Miki says PRC should be invited to a Vietnam peace conference		US govt allows Radio Corporation of America to remit $600,000 to PRC for telecommunications over past 18 years—ignored by PRC

24 Apr. Gaimushō reveals that, on instructions from Miki, unofficial contacts between Japan and PRC diplomats in Netherlands, Norway, Switzerland, and Laos have existed since beginning 1968

8 June. Chiang Kai-shek criticizes Japanese moves towards PRC. Abrogation of Yoshida Letter would mean scrapping Japan-ROC Peace Treaty

24 June. Vice-For. Min. Kurauchi says he has notified PRC, through Japanese diplomatic missions, that Japan is ready for talks designed to improve relations

July. US nationals can import Chinese goods worth $100

1969 *4 Apr.* MT Agreement extended for one year

Year	China (PRC)	Japan	Taiwan (ROC)	US/International
	29 Nov. Chou compares Satō with Tōjō	*13 Dec.* Cabinet Sec. Hori: Japan considering talks with PRC at ambassadorial level, similar to Sino-US talks		*22 Nov.* Satō-Nixon communiqué *Dec.* Further relaxations on US intercourse with China: foreign subsidiaries of US firms and US nationals abroad can trade with China
1970	*20 Mar.* Matsumura-Fujiyama mission to Peking *19 Apr.* MT Agreement extended for one year	*1 Sep.* Japan will allow teams participating in World Table Tennis Championships in Nagoya (1971) to use their official titles, even if from unrecognized states, i.e. PRC		*Mar.* US-PRC ambassadorial talks resumed in Warsaw

17 Nov. Japanese Ambassador to UN: Japan would welcome PRC but opposed to expulsion of Taiwan

3 Dec. Japan will not co-sponsor UN resolution designating Chinese representation as an 'important matter' in 1971

22 Jan. Satō refers to PRC by its official title for first time in a Diet policy speech

21 Feb. People's Daily indicates PRC will not enter into governmental contacts with Japan

1 Mar. MT Agreement extended for one year

15 Mar. For. Min. Aichi suggests two Chinas or one China—one Taiwan formula as solution of China problem

1971

Apr. Dollars permitted in trade settlements with China—part of 5-point policy to ease restrictions

Year	China (PRC)	Japan	Taiwan (ROC)	US/International
		20/21 July. Satō: KMT is 'legitimate' govt of China–Japan will not accept abolition of Treaty with ROC. Ready to go to Peking to normalize relations		*15 July.* Announcement of Nixon's trip to China
		July. MITI relaxes restrictions on trade with PRC		
		Aug. Kansai Dōyūkai becomes first economic organization to call for a one-China policy favouring PRC		
		Aug. Finance Ministry lowers tariffs on Chinese imports to levels applicable to other countries		
		25–30 Aug. Wang Kuo-chan attends Matsumura's funeral, meets Satō and other leaders		

Sep. Fuji and Mitsubishi Banks accept Chou's 4 Principles for trade—first banks to do so officially

22 Sep. Japan to co-sponsor US resolution seating PRC and ROC in UN and giving Security Council seat to PRC

Nov. C. Itoh accepts Chou's Principles on trade with PRC—first major trading house to do so

Nov. Big business mission from Japan goes to Peking

25 Dec. MT Agreement extended for one year

1972

23–7 Jan. Gromyko in Tokyo: Agreement to open negotiations for Russo-Japanese peace treaty in 1972

6 Mar. Gaimushō formulates 'Unified View' on China policy

15 May. Reversion of Okinawa

27 Feb. Nixon-Chou communiqué

Year	China (PRC)	Japan	Taiwan (ROC)	US/International
		16 May. Fukuda: Chou–Nixon communiqué means lapse of reference to Taiwan in Satō-Nixon communiqué (1969)		
			24 June. Japanese Ex.-Im. Bank lends $26 million to Taiwan	
		7 July. Tanaka becomes Prime Minister		
		19 July. Tanaka's first press conf.: fully 'understands' Chou's 3 principles for restoration of diplomatic relations		
		26 July. Authorization of Ex.-Im. Bank credit for sale of vinylon plant to PRC—Yoshida Letter (1964) considered as lapsed		
	Aug. Chou receives Takeiri (Kōmeitō) and backs Japanese claim to Northern Territories			
	Aug. Agreement on yuan/yen payments for trade and fixed rate of exchange			

Aug. Chou receives delegation from Mitsubishi Group

25–30 Sep. Tanaka visit to China – Chou-Tanaka communiqué (29 Sep.)

Nov. MT Agreement extended for one year

Aug. Chairman of Mitsubishi Heavy Industries visits Taiwan

30 Sep. Taiwan severs diplomatic relations with Japan

31 Aug.–1 Sep. Nixon-Tanaka meeting in Hawaii

21–4 Oct. Ōhira in Moscow – peace treaty negotiations not to start until 1973

1973

Jan. Semi-official relations established between Interchange Assoc. (Japan) and Assoc. of East Asian Relations (Taiwan)

Mar. 'Friendly Trade' system ended

Apr. Liao Cheng-chih heads mission to Japan

July. Japan protests against Chinese nuclear tests

10 Oct. Tanaka in Moscow

Nov. Kissinger visits Peking

1974   *3–6 Jan.* Ōhira in Peking – preliminary talks over peace treaty started

Year	China (PRC)	Japan	Taiwan (ROC)	US/International
		6 *Jan.* Three-year trade pact between Japan and China signed		
		20 *Apr.* Japan-China Civil Aviation Agreement signed		*Nov.* Ford-Brezhnev summit in Vladivostok
	Nov. Kissinger in Peking	9 *Dec.* Miki becomes Prime Minister		
1975	15 *Jan.* Hori visits Peking	3 *Feb.* Soviet amb. Troyanovsky warns Shiina (Vice-Pres. of LDP) against Sino-Japanese Treaty		15 *Jan.* For. Min. Miyazawa in Moscow
		July. Restoration of air links between Japan and Taiwan		
	15 *Aug.* Three-year Fisheries Agreement signed between China and Japan			
		Nov. Miyazawa enunciates Japan's 'Four Principles' over anti-hegemony clause		

1976 8 *Jan.* Death of Chou En-lai	9–13 *Jan.* Gromyko visit to Tokyo	
	1 *June.* Japan ratifies Non-Proliferation Treaty	
	9 *July.* Miyazawa says Chinese support over Northern Territories issue is unhelpful	
	12 *July.* Miyazawa states that Japan would not welcome any change in US-China relations that would mean abrogation of US-Taiwan Security Treaty	
17 *July.* Chinese abruptly postpone mission to Japan to discuss shipping		
18 *July.* Chinese attack Miyazawa statement on Northern Territories		
9 *Sep.* Death of Mao Tse-tung		
	24 *Dec.* Fukuda Takeo becomes Prime Minister	
1977		20 *Jan.* Inauguration of President Carter – US policy of gradual withdrawal of troops from South Korea

Bibliographical Note

It is hoped that the following list will be useful to those non-specialist readers who wish to undertake further study of some aspect of Japanese affairs. It is divided into the following sections: History; Social and Cultural Background; Postwar Politics and Economics; Postwar Foreign and Security Policy; China and Taiwan; the Press; Official Documents.

As in the main text and notes, the names of Japanese authors are given in Japanese style – with the family name before the given name.

HISTORY

Several excellent books offer a gateway into the study of Japan. Only three are mentioned here: E. O. Reischauer, *Japan Past and Present* (New York, Knopf, 1953) is a masterly summary of Japanese history from earliest times. G. R. Storry, *A History of Modern Japan* (Harmondsworth, Penguin Books, 1960), and W. G. Beasley, *The Modern History of Japan* (London, Weidenfeld & Nicolson, 1963) are quite detailed and very readable accounts of the more recent periods in the history of Japan.

The work of Sir George Sansom is in a class by itself. It may be approached through his *Japan: a Short Cultural History*, 2nd edn, 2nd imp. rev. (London, The Cresset Press, 1952) before one moves on to his monumental *A History of Japan*, published in three volumes (London, The Cresset Press, 1958, 1961, 1964 respectively), which takes the reader up to the Meiji Restoration. The subsequent period to the end of the nineteenth century is partly covered in his study of the interaction between Japanese culture and Western influences, *The Western World and Japan* (London, The Cresset Press, 1950). This book also contains an interesting general discussion of the relations between Europe and Asia up to the middle of the eighteenth century. Finally, Sansom has left a stimulating and suggestive essay, *Japan in World History* (London, George Allen & Unwin, 1952), based on a series of lectures delivered in Japan.

Before the reader turns his attention to the Meiji and post-Meiji periods, he may also wish to consult D. M. Brown, *Nationalism in Japan: an Introductory Historical Analysis* (Berkeley, University of California Press, 1955), which traces the subject back to Japan's very early history. H. Borton, *Japan's Modern Century* (New York, The Ronald Press, 1955) provides a general political and diplomatic history of modern Japan, and G. C. Allen, *A Short Economic History of Modern Japan*, 2nd rev. edn (London, Allen & Unwin, 1962) does the same in the economic field. Those wishing to pursue that subject in greater depth, should use W. W. Lockwood's very substantial *The Economic Development of Japan: Growth and Structural Change 1868–1938* (London, Oxford University Press, 1955).

The difficult and complex subject of Japan's modernization is dealt with in six symposia of a uniformly high standard, edited by distinguished scholars and published by Princeton University Press. They are, in order of appearance: M. B. Jansen, *Changing Japanese Attitudes towards Modernization* (1965); W. W. Lockwood, *The State and Economic Enterprise in Japan* (1965); R. P. Dore, *Aspects of Social Change in Modern Japan* (1967); R. E. Ward, *Political Development in Modern Japan* (1968); D. H. Shively, *Tradition and Modernization in Japanese Culture* (1971); J. W. Morley, *Dilemmas of Growth in Prewar Japan* (1971). The reader will find a stimulating discussion of the academic and theoretical problems involved in the study of tradition and modernization as they affect Japan in a review article by J. A. Whyte, 'Tradition and Politics in Studies of Contemporary Japan', *World Politics*, vol. XXVI, no. 3, April 1974, pp. 400–27.

Illuminating studies of Japan's foreign policy in the late nineteenth and early twentieth centuries are found in the two-volume history of the Anglo-Japanese Alliance by I. H. Nish, *The Anglo-Japanese Alliance: the Diplomacy of Two Island Empires, 1894–1907* and *Alliance in Decline: a Study in Anglo-Japanese Relations, 1908–1923* (London, The Athlone Press, 1968 and 1972 respectively); in H. Conroy, *The Japanese Seizure of Korea, 1869–1910* (London, Oxford University Press, 1961); and in M. B. Jansen, *The Japanese and Sun Yat-sen* (Cambridge, Mass., Harvard University Press, 1954), which is relevant for the subject matter of this book. Jansen's work may be supplemented by a collection of papers written by Sun Yat-sen and published under the title, *The Vital Problem of China* (Taipei, Chinese Cultural Service, 1953).

Japanese policy in China during the war of the 1930s and 1940s is described in John Hunter Boyle's substantial and absorbing *China and Japan at War, 1937–1945: the Politics of Collaboration* (Stanford, Calif., Stanford University Press, 1972). Lincoln Li, *The Japanese Army in North China 1937–1941: Problems of Political and Economic Control* (Tokyo, Oxford University Press, 1975) has a narrower focus but throws light on the Japanese 'contribution' to the rise of communism in that region.

Pre-war decision-making in Japan is revealed in Ike N., *Japan's Decision for War: Records of the 1941 Policy Conferences* (Stanford, Calif., Stanford University Press, 1967) and discussed by Hosoya C. in two articles: 'Japan's Decision for War in 1941', *Peace Research in Japan – 1967* (Tokyo, The Japan Peace Research Group), pp. 41–51 and 'Characteristics of the Foreign Policy Decision-making System in Japan', *World Politics*, vol. XXVI, no. 3, April 1974, pp. 353–69.

SOCIAL AND CULTURAL BACKGROUND

Many of the essays in the Princeton Series, mentioned in the previous section, also apply to the subject matter considered here.

Ruth Benedict, *The Chrysanthemum and the Sword: Patterns of Japanese Culture* (New York, Houghton Mifflin, 1946) is a classic which still provides valuable insights about Japanese attitudes and behaviour, despite much criticism of her work and the inevitable march of scholarship. Two contemporary studies of Japanese society by Japanese scholars should be read together: Nakane C., *Japanese Society* (London, Weidenfeld & Nicolson, 1970) and Ishida T., *Japanese Society* (New York, Random House, 1971).

A view of traditional values associated with the domination of the feudal warrior class may be obtained by reading Nitobe I., *Bushido: the Soul of Japan* (New York, Putnam, 1905) and Okakura K., *The Book of Tea* (New York, Duffield, 1921). For an interpretation of the national character by a social psychologist, the reader might turn to Minami H., *Psychology of the Japanese People* (Tokyo, University of Tokyo Press, 1971). For an interesting example of how the Japanese see themselves and the kind of book which excites their interest, see the best-seller, I. Ben-Dasan, *The Japanese and the Jews* (New York and Tokyo, Weatherhill, 1972). The mystery of the author's identity adds to the book's popularity. There is strong evidence that he is Japanese.

The place of intellectuals and their relationship to society is dealt with by Arima T., *The Failure of Freedom: a Portrait of Modern Japanese Intellectuals* (Cambridge, Mass., Harvard University Press, 1969). The work of one of the most influential among contemporary Japanese scholars and intellectuals may be sampled in Maruyama M., *Thought and Behaviour in Modern Japanese Politics* (London, Oxford University Press, 1969). Of special interest in connection with the theme of the present book is the recently published collection of short essays by Katō S., *The Japan-China Phenomenon: Conflict or Compatibility?* (London, Paul Norbury, 1974). It contains many interesting observations on the cultural relationship between the two countries.

POSTWAR POLITICS AND ECONOMICS

Decision-making processes have been the subject of much scholarly discussion. A recent contribution, Ezra Vogel, ed., *Modern Japanese Organization and Decision Making* (Berkeley, University of California Press, 1975), takes a critical look at some popular assumptions.

An excellent cluster of studies introduces the reader to various aspects of Japanese politics since World War II. H. Baerwald deals with the parliamentary system in his admirably succinct and informative *Japan's Parliament: an Introduction* (London, Cambridge University Press, 1974). The party system as a whole is discussed in R. A. Scalapino and Masumi J., *Parties and Politics in Contemporary Japan* (Berkeley, University of California

Press, 1962). The LDP is the subject of an excellent study by Fukui H., *Party in Power: the Japanese Liberal-Democrats and Policy-making* (Berkeley, University of California Press, 1970), which has a particularly useful section on the party's attitudes towards China. Another study of the LDP is by N. B. Thayer, *How the Conservatives rule Japan* (Princeton, NJ, Princeton University Press, 1969). The left wing is the subject of A. B. Cole, G. O. Totten, and Uyehara C. H., *Socialist Parties in Postwar Japan* (New Haven, Conn., Yale University Press, 1966). The attitude of the JSP on foreign affairs is well covered by J. A. A. Stockwin, *The Japanese Socialist Party and Neutralism: a Study of a Political Party and its Foreign Policy* (London, Cambridge University Press, 1968); this author also examines the general political scene in his more recent *Japan: Divided Politics in a Growth Economy* (London, Weidenfeld & Nicolson, 1975). The JCP is the subject of R. A. Scalapino, *The Japanese Communist Movement: 1920–1966* (Berkeley, University of California Press, 1967).

There are two illuminating case studies of the domestic political process in relation to issues of external policy. D. C. Hellmann, *Japanese Foreign Policy and Domestic Politics: the Peace Agreement with the Soviet Union* (Berkeley, University of California Press, 1969) and G. R. Packard, *Protest in Tokyo: the Security Treaty Crisis of 1960* (Princeton, NJ, Princeton University Press, 1966).

An early explanation of Japan's 'economic miracle' may be found in *Consider Japan* (London, Duckworth, 1963), by a group of correspondents of *The Economist*. A. Maddison has a very stimulating interpretation of Japan's phenomenal growth in his comparative study, *Economic Growth in Japan and the USSR* (London, Allen & Unwin, 1969). G. C. Allen, *Japan's Place in Trade Strategy: Larger Role in Pacific Region* (London, The Atlantic Trade Study, July 1968) deals with the postwar pattern of trade. Yanaga C., *Big Business in Japanese Politics* (New Haven, Conn., Yale University Press, 1968) deals with economic pressure groups but concentrates on big business organizations.

POSTWAR FOREIGN AND SECURITY POLICY

Among the best general interpretations of Japan's place in the postwar world is R. Guillain, *Japon, Troisième Grand* (Paris, Editions du Seuil, 1969), which has appeared in P. O'Brian's translation as *The Japanese Challenge* (London, Hamilton, 1970). F. C. Langdon, *Japan's Foreign Policy* (Vancouver, University of British Columbia Press, 1973) is a general study of Japan's external relations since 1960. An interesting account of Japan's foreign and security policies is to be found in J. K. Emmerson, *Arms, Yen & Power: the Japanese Dilemma* (New York, Dunellen, 1971), the author being a former US foreign service officer with considerable experience of Japan. For a Japanese view of the first decade after the war, see Yoshida S., *The Yoshida Memoirs* (London, Heinemann, 1961), an abbreviated translation by Yoshida Kenichi of the autobiography of the Japanese statesman who dominated the political scene until the mid-fifties.

Several general studies have appeared in recent years, speculating about the future course of Japanese policy. H. Kahn, *The Emerging Japanese Super-state: Challenge and Response* (Englewood Cliffs, NJ, Prentice-Hall, 1970) was one of the first and most controversial. More recent books have included Z. Brzezinski, *The Fragile Blossom, Crisis and Change in Japan* (New York, Harper & Row, 1972); D. C. Hellmann, *Japan and East Asia: the New International Order* (London, Pall Mall Press, 1972); and J. Morley, ed., *Forecast for Japan: Security in the Seventies* (Princeton, NJ, Princeton University Press, 1972).

The study by Chae-Jin Lee, *Japan Faces China: Political and Economic Relations in the Postwar Era* (The Johns Hopkins University Press, Baltimore, Md, 1976) came to my attention too late to be used in the preparation of the present book. The chapter by Matsumoto S., 'Japan and China: Domestic and Foreign Influences on Japan's Policy', in A. Halpern, ed., *Policies Towards China* (New York, McGraw-Hill, 1965, pp. 123–64) is a good introduction to relations with China. Shao-chuan Leng, *Japan and Communist China* (Kyoto, Dōshisha University Press, 1958) deals with the problems of the 1950s. This may be followed by K. E. Shaw's informative *Japan's China Problem: Marginal Position and Attitude during the Ikeda Period* (Tokyo, International Christian University, April 1968), but this is very difficult reading because of its extraordinary use of English. Etō S., 'Japan and China – a New Stage?' (*Problems of Communism*, US Information Agency, vol. XXI, no. 6, Nov–Dec 1972, pp. 1–17) is a useful interpretative essay about the normalization of relations between the two countries. For the background and practice of trade with China up to 1972, the handbook published by the Japan External Trade Organization (JETRO), *How to Approach the China Market* (Tokyo, Press International Ltd., 1972) is useful.

Outstanding among the many books dealing with Japanese-American relations is E. O. Reischauer, *The United States and Japan* (Cambridge, Mass., Harvard University Press, 1965). R. Clough, *East Asia and U.S. Security* (Washington, D.C., The Brookings Institution, 1975) speculates about the relationship after the withdrawal from Southeast Asia, mainly from the American point of view. A similar discussion, more strictly focused on defence problems, occurs in R. Osgood, *The Weary and the Wary: U.S. and Japanese Security Policies in Transition* (Baltimore, Md, The Johns Hopkins University Press, 1972).

Japan's relations with Southeast Asia have been dealt with in L. Olson, *Japan in Postwar Asia* (New York, Praeger for the Council on Foreign Relations, 1970) and in Hellmann, *Japan and East Asia*, mentioned earlier in this section.

M. E. Weinstein has written a short pioneering study on Japan's re-armament, *Japanese Postwar Defense Policy: 1947–68* (New York, Columbia University Press, 1971). Emmerson's *Arms, Yen & Power* (this section, above) also contains much useful material on Japanese defence policy. The nuclear question is very carefully examined by John E. Endicott in *Japan's Nuclear Option: Political, Technical, and Strategic Factors* (New York, Praeger, 1975). A specific aspect of this problem is discussed in J. Welfield, *Japan and Nuclear China: Japanese Reactions to China's Nuclear Weapons* (Canberra, Australian National University Press, 1970). Up-to-date information about Japan's defence effort is found in the annual editions of *The Military Balance* (London, The International Institute for Strategic Studies) and useful background articles frequently appear in the annual editions of *Strategic Survey* by the same Institute. It has also published a number of occasional papers relevant to our present study, mostly by Japanese authors. Noteworthy among them are Rōyama M., *The Asian Balance of Power: a Japanese View* (Adelphi Paper no. 42, Nov 1967), R. Ellingworth, *Japanese Economic Policies and Security* (Adelphi Paper no. 90, October 1972), Muraoka K., *Japanese Security and the United States* (Adelphi Paper no. 95, Feb 1973), Kosaka M., *Options for Japan's Foreign Policy* (Adelphi Paper no. 97, Summer 1973).

CHINA AND TAIWAN

Perhaps the best introduction to the Chinese perspective is to be found in C. P. Fitzgerald, *The Chinese View of Their Place in the World* (London, Oxford University Press for the Royal Institute of International Affairs, 1969). From there one should proceed to the symposium edited by J. K. Fairbank, *The Chinese World Order: Traditional China's Foreign Relations* (Cambridge, Mass., Harvard University Press, 1968). J. R. Levenson, *Confucian China and its Modern Fate: the Problem of Intellectual Continuity* (London, Routledge & Kegan Paul, 1958) is a brilliant study of the intellectual revolution in modern China. A good discussion of Confucian concepts and their practical application is to be found in M. F. Nelson, *Korea and the Old Orders in Eastern Asia* (Baton Rouge, Louisiana State University Press, 1946).

The origins and roots of the Chinese communist movement may be examined through S. Schram's masterly biography, *Mao Tse-tung* (Harmondsworth, Penguin Books, 1970). It should be supplemented with B. Schwartz, *Chinese Communism and the Rise of Mao* (Cambridge, Mass., Harvard University Press, 1951) and E. Snow, *Red Star over China* (New York, Grove Press, 1968). Two interpretations of the foreign policy of the People's Republic of China are provided by I. Ojha, *Chinese Foreign Policy in an Age of Transition: the Diplomacy of Cultural Despair* (Boston, Mass., Beacon Press, 1969) and H. Hinton, *China's Turbulent Quest* (New York, Macmillan, 1970). Speculation about future trends is the theme of A. D. Barnett, *Uncertain Passage: China's Transition to the Post-Mao Era* (Washington, D.C., The Brookings Institution, 1974). Chinese defence policy is also treated in the publications of the International Institute for Strategic Studies. The nuclear question is discussed by H. Gelber in *Nuclear Weapons and Chinese Policy* (Adelphi Paper no. 99, Summer 1973).

For Taiwan, the reader is referred to the collection of short studies edited by M. Mancall, *Formosa Today* (New York, Praeger, 1964) and to Lung-chu Chen and H. Lasswell, *Formosa, China and the United Nations: Formosa in the World Community* (New York, St. Martin's Press, 1967) which presents a particular point of view about the future of the island.

THE PRESS

There are four English-language dailies in Japan. *The Japan Times* caters exclusively for foreign readers and Japanese who wish to read English. It also publishes *The Japan Times Weekly*, which carries the main news of the week and some analytical background articles. The three major vernacular national papers all have English editions: *The Mainichi Daily News*, *The Asahi Evening News*, and the *Yomiuri* include articles translated from their Japanese language editions and thus convey something of the flavour of Japanese politics and the kind of material that helps to form public opinion.

The US Embassy in Tokyo provides regular translations and summaries from the daily press and a monthly survey of magazines, which includes full translations and abstracts. They are invaluable sources but not easy to obtain as they have a limited circulation.

Among Japanese journals published in English, *The Japan Interpreter*, published by the Japan Center for International Exchange, carries scholarly articles on all aspects of Japanese life and thought, and social criticism, both of a high standard, some written specifically for the journal, others translated from Japanese sources. The *Japan Quarterly*, published by *Asahi Shimbun*, is more a literary and cultural magazine although it includes commentaries on current affairs and general articles about political, economic, and social problems. It has a useful chronology of events. A new quarterly, the *Japan Echo*, appeared in 1974. It publishes full or summarized translations of articles dealing with Japan's social, political, and economic problems, as well as some devoted to international affairs.

Among foreign publications which provide a steady stream of material on Japan, the *Far Eastern Economic Review* brings background articles on a weekly basis. *Asian Survey*, published monthly by the University of California Press, and *Pacific Affairs*, published quarterly by the University of British Columbia, include more scholarly and interpretative essays.

OFFICIAL DOCUMENTS

A number of Japanese official documents are available in English, including *Diplomatic Bluebooks*, the annual *Statistical Survey of Japan's Economy*, important policy speeches, and occasional documents dealing with every aspect of Japanese affairs. They are published by government departments, and may be obtained through the information departments of Japanese embassies.

Index